Stuart Harris-Logan
(Photo: Robert McFadzean)

STUART HARRIS-LOGAN is the Keeper of Archives and Collections at the Royal Conservatoire of Scotland. Stuart joined the Royal Conservatoire in 2009 and was tasked with creating the institution's archive from the mess of old store cupboards. What emerged was an impressive collection of materials covering the full span of the Conservatoire's 175-year history. The archive has grown and flourished to become the busiest conservatoire archive in the UK, with one of the largest collections of historic musical instruments in the world.

Royal Conservatoire of Scotland

Raising the Curtain

STUART HARRIS-LOGAN

Luath Press Limited
EDINBURGH
www.luath.co.uk

First published 2021

ISBN 978-1-910022-76-4 limited edition hardback
ISBN 978-1-910022-77-1 hardback
ISBN 978-1-910022-78-8 paperback

The author's right to be identified as author of this book
under the Copyright, Designs and Patents Act 1988 has been asserted.

The paper used in this book is recyclable. It is made
from low chlorine pulps produced in a low energy,
low emissions manner from renewable forests.

Printed and bound by
Grafo S.A., Bilbao

Typeset in 11 point Sabon and 9.5 point Avenir Next
by Main Point Books, Edinburgh

Images © Royal Conservatoire of Scotland unless otherwise stated
Text © Royal Conservatoire of Scotland 2021

Contents

'Dear Student' by Jackie Kay   8

Foreword by HRH The Prince Charles   11

Foreword by Sir Cameron Mackintosh   13

Introduction by Professor Jeffrey Sharkey   15

Prelude   19

Timeline   21

1. Rational Recreation   25
2. Education for All   33
3. First Steps   43
4. Moving   51
5. Athenaeum School of Music   57
6. Active Society for the Propagation of Contemporary Music   69
7. Playing On   75
   SPOTLIGHT: Tommy Smith   78
   SPOTLIGHT: Pamella Dow   83
8. Making a Drama   85
   SPOTLIGHT: John Cairney   90

	SPOTLIGHT: Jackie Kay	93
	SPOTLIGHT: David Tennant	95
	SPOTLIGHT: James McAvoy	98
	SPOTLIGHT: Ros Steen	104
	SPOTLIGHT: Alan Cumming	108
	SPOTLIGHT: Aaron Lee Lambert	112
	SPOTLIGHT: Richard Madden	115
	SPOTLIGHT: Ncuti Gatwa	117
9	One Conservatoire	123
	SPOTLIGHT: Maggie Kinloch	124
10	Premières	131
	SPOTLIGHT: Tony Osoba	132
	SPOTLIGHT: Isobel 'Bunty' Fowler	136
	SPOTLIGHT: Karen Cargill	145
	SPOTLIGHT: Johnny McKnight	149
	SPOTLIGHT: Jamie Reid	152
	SPOTLIGHT: Ciaran Stewart	156
11	What's in a Name?	161
	SPOTLIGHT: Maura Coll	163
	SPOTLIGHT: John Wallace	171
12	Change is a Constant	175
	Coda	177
	A Note on Source Materials	189
	Acknowledgements	191

*This book is dedicated to all students
of the Arts, past, present and future*

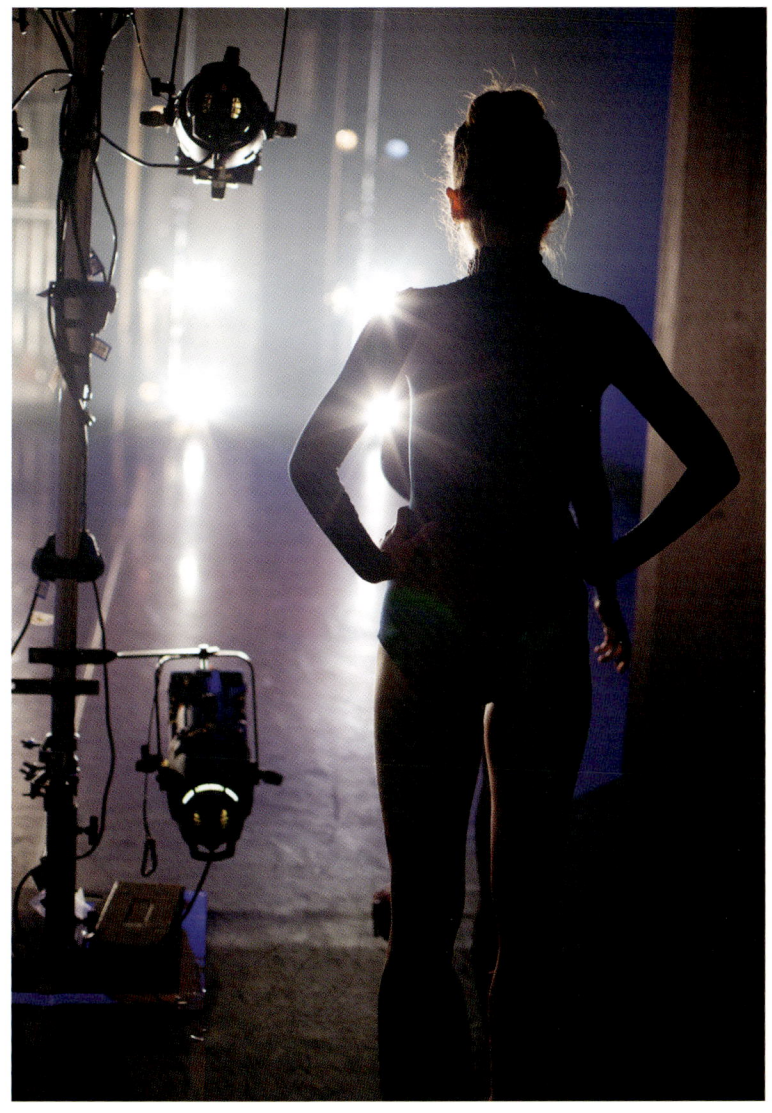

A dancer waits in the wings of the New Athenaeum Theatre stage as she
prepares to perform in the BA Modern Ballet Graduation Showcase, 2015
(Photo: KK Dundas)

Dear Student

There was plenty speech and drama
on the streets of Glasgow
when I was a new young building
cried Athenaeum;
and South of me, the river Clyde
called with its ships,
opened its dark arms to builders, fitters, engineers.
But I was all for music and dance,
the fine romance of a Shakespeare play,
the beat of a Burns ballad;
all for art and design.
Dear Student, I wanted to make you mine.

All my life I've rung the changes,
a bell ringer on the hours,
joy to sorrow, red brick to pale stone,
Buchanan Street to Renfrew.
I've watched as talent grew and grew,
changed my name again and again,
from Academy to Academy, College, back to Academy.
Years: I've seen the glittering attire, the show stoppers,
the troupers, the blootered, the curtain rise and fall…
One star turn comes, goes, comes and goes.
I've seen it all. I've been it all.
I've been to the Panto. Oh No I haven't! I've been to the ball.

So, what's in a name? See me –
the Royal Scottish Academy of Music
when the country was at war.
Then Vaudeville, tableau, opera, pas de chat, pas de bas,
and now curtains up on my newest name,
the Royal Conservatoire of Scotland,
today on the 3rd of October 2011.
One shining girl waits in the wings.
One rising star stands up and sings.
Time again, the changes rings.
Dear Student, the gifts that talent brings!
You tap on the silvery light of the moon,
on the stars, on the silver screen,
all you'll be or have ever been coming here soon.

'Dear Student' by Jackie Kay was commissioned in 2011 to mark the change of name to Royal Conservatoire of Scotland.

His Royal Highness, The Prince Charles, Duke of Rothesay, at Birkhall, 2020
(Photo: Katrina Farquhar)

HRH THE PRINCE CHARLES, DUKE OF ROTHESAY

For a hundred and seventy-five years, the Royal Conservatoire of Scotland has nurtured the finest talent, fostered the most glittering careers and brought endless prestige to Scotland.

In celebrating this remarkable anniversary, I am delighted, as Patron, to join the students, staff and alumni of this world-leading institution in celebrating what has been an extraordinary record of achievement.

Scarcely can the founders of the Glasgow Athenaeum have imagined the success with which their endeavours would be crowned, or the many and varied forms in which the performing arts are now expressed. They would, however, surely recognise the timeless and joyous qualities of creativity that make the arts an essential part of being human, and they would, I am sure, rejoice to see the way the Conservatoire has fulfilled their aims so splendidly.

As we mark this great milestone, we give thanks for those who, over so many years, have built this great international centre. We celebrate, too, the outstanding talents of the present generation and we look forward to those days, still to come, when the arts and artists will, in new ways, continue to connect, to inspire and to transform.

Sir Cameron Mackintosh
(Photo: Tolga Akmen/*Chicago Tribune*)

Foreword

I consider myself very lucky that the performing arts, in particular musical theatre, have defined my life.

It is through the miraculous alchemy of music, words and movement that we tell and share our stories. It allows us to reflect backwards, gaze forwards and glance sideways and, perhaps most importantly of all, allows us to create an essential connection with each other. To be part of this coming together, to be able to add magic to it through stage design, creating an atmosphere, or generating a moment of drama, is the privilege of all of us in the arts. It is our passion and pride.

As President of the Royal Conservatoire of Scotland, I am proud to join in celebrating the 175 years throughout which this institution has been a powerhouse of the arts, both in Scotland and internationally. If recent times have shown us anything, it is that we need our arts and artists more than ever. Yes, for our economies, but also for our wellbeing, for the essence of our souls. We need people to continue helping us tell our stories; artists and creative citizens of the future who, in turn, inspire both their colleagues and audiences through their imagination. This is such a place and my congratulations to the RCS on its first 175 years. May it continue to grow from strength to strength and keep helping us tell stories to each other and to the world.

Sir Cameron Mackintosh
President, Royal Conservatoire of Scotland

Professor Jeffrey Sharkey, Principal of the Royal Conservatoire of Scotland, pictured in 2020
(Photo: Robert McFadzean)

Introduction

I WAS REPRESENTING the Peabody Institute of Johns Hopkins University in Baltimore at the Annual Association of European Conservatoires (AEC) Congress in Valencia. I ran into John Wallace, then principal of the Royal Scottish Academy of Music and Drama (RSAMD), whom I knew from his time as Head of Brass at the Royal Academy of Music. We sat down for a beer, exchanging stories about our respective institutions. When John described the tremendous growth in the performing arts at RSAMD, so much so that a name change was mooted, I said to myself that I needed to learn more about this northern latitude cultural powerhouse.

Some years later, I was honoured to be selected as John's successor as Principal of the then recently renamed Royal Conservatoire of Scotland. I beat a path to its door because it spanned all of the performing arts, it was deeply connected to its own nation while being proudly international and European and it was trying to grapple with some key questions: what is next? Who are the arts for? How should we educate for the future? My colleagues and I live with these questions on a daily basis, and being unafraid to pose them, keen to learn and excited to collaborate has propelled us to the forefront of higher education in music, both in our country and in the wider world.

Conservatoires were a 19th century invention designed to serve specific needs in music, largely for performance in bands and orchestras. They became expert in these areas – but at some cost; by focusing on excellent recreations of an existing repertoire, they left out the creative side of composing, improvising, arranging and producing. Traditional and jazz musicians never stopped working in these areas, but classical musicians lost some skills that their forbears, before the invention of conservatoires, took for granted. I am happy to say that all of our musicians, actors, dancers, filmmakers and production students now balance recreation with creation, making them more adaptable artists to help shape the profession.

The RCS is proud to be a 'national' conservatoire with international ambitions. We take our convening role within Scotland seriously, contributing to instrumental and classroom training in music, drama and dance for all ages. We are proud to have contributed to a major change in government policy in 2021 which made music lessons free for all children in Scotland.

The combination of being rooted in our own soil and open to the world has made us an increasingly attractive destination for international students. Currently, we have students from more than 60 countries studying at RCS. It is a never-ending delight to see how the arts build bridges between different cultures and backgrounds, with all students united in their desire to discover something beyond themselves as they strive for excellence in their chosen art.

The story of this place, now known as the Royal Conservatoire of Scotland, has never been about bricks or mortar, dates or statistics. It's always been about people: staff, students and a wider family of alumni, supporters, partners and friends. And, collectively, their responsive ideas, their dedication and their dreams.

The RCS proudly reflects its home city of Glasgow in the belief that the arts are for everyone. Our founders' vision was to provide artistic education for those social classes that might not have been able to progress to higher education. We seek to reduce labels and barriers and create a cultural fluidity that will influence the performing arts in positive and inclusive directions.

As we mark our 175th anniversary, we seek to celebrate our

founding principles and adapt them to a climate-aware pandemic recovery. One that uses the arts to recreate some of the fractured bonds of society and create the 'collective effervescence' (as Emile Durkheim puts it) that we experience with live performing arts.

Professor Jeffrey Sharkey
Principal

Contemporary Performance Practice student Fionnuala OfMaura performs her piece *Carelessness Causes Fire* during the Propel Festival at Jupiter Artland, 2021 (Photo: Robert McFadzean)

Prelude

THE ROYAL CONSERVATOIRE OF SCOTLAND was founded as the Glasgow Athenaeum in 1847. Its founders envisioned that it would be an 'ornament' to the city, providing what we would now call further education to people of all backgrounds and situations for a moderate fee. 175 years later, it has come a long way; from a private members' club with classes in modern languages, logic and mathematics (and the occasional visiting lecturer) to a world-class conservatoire, the only one in the UK to provide training in all the major schools of the performing arts.

This book is part history, part celebration. The rich and extensive archives of the Royal Conservatoire of Scotland have provided some of the backstory, but equally important are the voices of those who have come through our doors and lived the experience of our national school for the performing arts. For every person included here there are hundreds, if not thousands, more whose stories, though similar, are their own, and it has not been possible to include them all. As a history, this book is illustrative, not exhaustive. As a celebration, it is inclusive and forward-looking.

175 years are too many to adequately commit to paper. Inevitably some things will have to be missed out entirely, and others only glossed over; equally there will be some names which are conspicuous by their absence. These omissions are almost inevitable in any book of this kind, and it is important to note that a lack of inclusion does not equate to a lack of consequence. Emily Dickinson wrote 'tell all the truth but tell it slant'. This is only part of the story.

The following seems an unlikely fable, retold so often in the folklore of the institution that it has begun to stretch credulity. It reads almost like an alternative to the butterfly effect in Chaos Theory, whereby a lone butterfly flapping its wings in New Mexico can eventually cause a tornado in China. In our case, the butterfly is a different kind of flyer, and the tornado is the creation of an internationally recognised institution devoted to the liberal arts and sciences which, at the point of opening, could boast over 1,600 members.

Improbable as it may seem, it's perfectly true.

Timeline

1847   The provisional Glasgow Athenaeum committee met on 18 January to discuss founding the institution in Steel's Coffee House, Argyle Street, Glasgow.

1847   Glasgow Athenaeum Opening Soirée held on 28 December at the City Halls, presided over by Charles Dickens.
The Glasgow Athenaeum is formally opened in the Assembly Rooms on Ingram Street, Glasgow.

1848   On 14 February, Ralph Waldo Emerson delivers his first lecture in the City Hall, under the auspices of the Glasgow Athenaeum.

1848   On 27 September, Chopin gives one of his last concerts a few doors down from the Athenaeum in the Merchants' Hall, Hutcheson Street.

1885   Glasgow Athenaeum becomes a Limited Company: the Glasgow Athenaeum Ltd.

1886   Glasgow Athenaeum begins teaching acting and elocution.

1888   Glasgow Athenaeum moves from the Assembly Rooms to purpose-built accommodation on St George's Place (now Nelson Mandela Place). The old entrance to the Assembly Rooms is preserved as the arch at the western entrance to Glasgow Green and some of the frontage is preserved in the Briggait.
At this time the Athenaeum Commercial College splits to eventually become part of the University of Strathclyde.

1890   Glasgow Athenaeum School of Music is established under Allan Macbeth, graduate of the Leipzig Conservatorium, with the remit of establishing a more European style of conservatoire education in Glasgow.

1891 Glasgow Athenaeum holds a supper for Henry Irving, the first actor to receive a knighthood for services to drama, at which Buffalo Bill Cody and Bram Stoker are also present.

1891/2 Emma Ritter-Bondy is appointed Professor of Piano, the first woman in the UK to be awarded a professorship.

1900 A new issue of 10,000 £1 shares is made to raise money to extend the building and facilities.

1904 Andrew Carnegie appointed Vice President of the Glasgow Athenaeum (a position he occupied until his death in 1919). Henri Verbrugghen, a graduate of the Brussels Conservatorium, is appointed violin teacher and de facto Head of Strings of the Athenaeum School of Music.

1927 The Glasgow Athenaeum Ltd. becomes the Scottish National Academy of Music.

1928 On 29 March, William Gillies Whittaker (after whom the Library is named, as he raised funds from the Carnegie Foundation to establish a 'proper' library) is appointed Principal of the SNAM and Gardiner Chair of Music at the University of Glasgow (the two positions being concurrent).

1929 Erik Chisholm (Glasgow Athenaeum School of Music alumnus) establishes the Active Society for the Propagation of Contemporary Music which over the following eight years brings composers, including Bartók, Hindemith and Sorabji, to perform in Glasgow.

1941 Sir Ernest Bullock (aka Deadly Ernest) appointed Principal of the SNAM and Gardiner Chair of Music.

1943 Citizens Theatre founded by dramatist and screenwriter James Bridie, who later founds the College of Dramatic Art. For the first two years of its life, the Citizens Theatre operates out of the SNAM/RSAM Athenaeum Theatre.

TIMELINE

1944 On 30 December, the Scottish National Academy of Music becomes the Royal Scottish Academy of Music under the patronage of Queen Elizabeth the Queen Consort, later the Queen Mother.

1947 The Sibelius Prize is established after funds raised to support the composer Jean Sibelius during the Second World War are not permitted to leave the country. Sibelius approves the endowment of an essay prize in his name.

1948 Glaswegian pianist and composer Frederic Lamond, the second-last surviving pupil of Liszt, dies on 21 February. His final years were spent teaching and performing at the RSAM.

1950 The College of Dramatic Art is founded by James Bridie under the direction of Colin Chandler. John Cairney is the first student across the threshold.

1953 Dr Henry Havergal becomes Principal of the RSAM and Gardiner Chair of Music after Sir Ernest Bullock leaves to take up the post of Principal of the Royal College of Music.

1962 RSAM's College of Dramatic Art becomes the first British drama school to have a broadcast-specification television studio.

1965 Cecil Williams, an anti-apartheid campaigner who helped Nelson Mandela escape from South Africa, is appointed to the teaching staff in the College of Dramatic Art.

1968 On 13 March, RSAM becomes Royal Scottish Academy of Music and Drama (RSAMD).
Degree courses validated by Glasgow University are established.

1969 Sir Kenneth Barritt appointed Principal of RSAMD.

1976 Sir David Lumsden appointed Principal of RSAMD.

1982 Sir Philip Ledger appointed Principal of RSAMD after Sir David Lumsden appointed Principal of the Royal Academy of Music.

1993 Degree-awarding powers granted to RSAMD by the Privy Council, making it the first conservatoire in the UK to attain this status.

1987 Renfrew Street building completed and RSAMD moves there from Buchanan Street/St George's Place.

1988 Official opening of the Renfrew Street building by The Queen Mother on 9 March.

1998 The Alexander Gibson Opera School (AGOS) opens – the first purpose-built opera school in Britain.

2000 First research students recruited.

2001 John Wallace CBE appointed Principal of the RSAMD.

2002 Death of Royal Patron, The Queen Mother.
HRH The Duke of Rothesay becomes patron.

2009 Ballet and Jazz degrees added to the curriculum.

2010 Wallace Studios at Speirs Locks is acquired and converted to ballet and production space originally known as Speirs Locks Studios.

2011 On 1 September, name changed from RSAMD to Royal Conservatoire of Scotland.

2014 Jeffrey Sharkey appointed Principal of RCS.

2016 The QS World University Rankings include the performing arts for the first time. RCS is voted third in the world for performing arts education. RCS has consistently performed in the top tier of schools ever since.

2020 COVID-19 forces the campus to close for the longest time in the institution's history. Learning and teaching continue online, with a gradual move to blended learning (a mixture of in-person and online) as conditions permit.

I

Rational Recreation

ON 18 JANUARY 1847, a group of 25 citizens of Glasgow squeezed themselves into Steel's Coffee House on one of the city's busiest thoroughfares. It was a Monday, and – being January – if it wasn't raining then it was probably snowing.

The Victorian coffee house was a hangover from the 17th and 18th centuries. In those days, the coffee house was seen as the home of intellectual discussion and political debate; a meeting place where business could be transacted, contracts agreed and resolutions made over a table of steaming 'dishes' of coffee. In Oxford, they earned the name 'penny universities', a title born from both their famous penny admission charge and their reputation as homes for thinkers, inventors, scholars, writers, innovators and artists. It was coffee that stoked the engine of the Age of Enlightenment.

It must have been with a sense of some importance, then, that our 25 highly caffeinated committee members met to lend their names and their time to, in their own words:

> Consider the propriety of endeavouring to form a Literary and Scientific Institution adapted to [...] the following features, viz. 1st Classes for studying systematically the more important departments of knowledge, including the modern languages, and other branches bearing directly on business. 2nd Short Courses of popular lectures. 3rd Reading Rooms and Library. 4th Essay and Discussion Classes. 5th

Gymnasium and Maths. 6th Occasional Concerts, Soirees etc. 7th Coffee Rooms.
(RCS Archives & Collections, Glasgow Athenaeum Minute Books, Vol. 1, p. 10)

Under this slew of Victorian verbiage, it is just about possible to discern that the meeting was about the formation of an institute of learning for what was then known as 'rational recreation'. That is, the theory that the acquisition of knowledge could be an end in itself and needn't be taught in a formal academic setting.

The scene is quite easy to imagine: lofty ideas mingling at once with the smoke and the impressive facial hair that the speakers, rapt by animated and idealistic discussions, no doubt sported. But how did it all come about?

The mythology surrounding the foundation of many old institutions is often to be taken with a pinch of salt, or at least a healthy awareness of romanticisation. In this case, however, we have a rare piece of provenance. Preserved in the archives of the Royal Conservatoire of Scotland is an original account of the founding impetus of the institution, written by those present at the time and still alive to approve the written version of events.

We should let them tell the story:

In the month of November, 1845, a young lad attended the introductory lecture to a course on Chemistry being delivered in the Andersonian University by Professor Penny. On leaving the lecture-room there was handed to him, in common with the rest of the audience, a circular entitled 'Glasgow Educational Association'. This circular he took home, and it afterwards fell into the hands of his elder brother. To this apparently trivial incident is to be directly traced the origin of the Glasgow Athenaeum. The lad in question was James Provan. (Lauder, *The Glasgow Athenaeum: A Sketch of Fifty Years' Work (1847–1897*, pp. 1–2)

RATIONAL RECREATION

Company Limited by Guarantee, and having a Capital Divided into Shares. Not for Gain.

THE GLASGOW ATHENÆUM (INCORPORATED.)

Incorporated under the Companies Acts 1862-98.

Only 16 at the time, James Provan was the younger brother of Moses Provan, a bibliophile who had begun his working life in the book trade before qualifying as a chartered accountant. The circular he so fortuitously chanced upon began:

> There are in Glasgow many young men eager to become more useful in society, but who […] feel themselves unqualified; and, however desirous they may be to obtain the requisite knowledge, are unable to do so from the fact that the present academical and other means of instruction are, in general, conducted not so much with a view to those who are engaged in business as to those whose time and energies are devoted to the acquisition of learning. The consequence is, that among the many who feel anxious to obtain a better education, few can do anything towards that end. (Lauder, *Athenaeum*, Appendix 1)

It is widely believed that Scotland introduced the second ever universal and compulsory education system in the world by virtue of the Education (Scotland) act of 1872. The first, if you were wondering, was in ancient Sparta. In the 1840s, however, there was no such system, and so the burgeoning mercantile expansion of Glasgow at this time brought a boom to the economy which saw no concomitant rise in the educational provision for the growing population. Put simply, there were a lot of wealthy young people, unqualified for any trade, with a lot of time on their hands. Moses Provan was clearly alive to the problem and immediately threw his hat in the ring alongside the writers of the flyer that his younger brother had discarded.

As a result of their efforts, the Glasgow Commercial College was born, meeting in the rooms of the Andersonian University on George Street later that year. It was not a success, and after only two sessions the Commercial College folded. Moses Provan, who had been treasurer of the ill-fated college, was not deterred. To him the problem was not a lack of want, but a want of means. The Commercial College had been conceived too modestly, and the institution he had in mind was much larger. In a fiery speech delivered as the Commercial College was beginning to decline, Moses Provan argued:

> If […] we had a large building, with spacious apartments, handsomely furnished; if we had therein a news-room, a reading-room, a library, all well supplied; if we had a comfortable coffee-room, a gymnasium, and baths; if we had not only classes for the talented and persevering few, but also popular lectures for the many, and concerts and other means of relaxation for all: should we not have the very thing that Glasgow stands in need of, an Institution of which the city might well be proud? (Lauder, *Athenaeum*, p. 5)

His argument carried the day, and on 18 January 1847 we find him with 24 of his fellow citizens in Steel's Coffee House, laying the intellectual foundations of what would become the Glasgow Athenaeum.

The name 'Athenaeum' was a deliberate reference to similar private members' clubs elsewhere in the United Kingdom, particularly London (est 1824), Liverpool (est 1797) and Manchester (est 1835). The word itself comes to us via classical Greece and the goddess

Athena, goddess of wisdom, which speaks well to their shared aim of the 'advancement and diffusion of knowledge'.

In February 1847, Moses Provan put forward a prospectus for the Glasgow Athenaeum:

> […] the promoters of the Glasgow Athenaeum indulge the hope that the time has arrived at which it may be submitted to their fellow citizens, whether by the judicious consolidation of schemes that are now distinct, and the willing co-operation of the many enlightened and philanthropic men, where efforts are at present isolated, a great Popular Institute might not be formed capable of powerfully advancing the mental culture of all classes of the community, and which, through its comprehensiveness, efficiency, and liberality, might not unworthily be spoken of as one of the most honourable and distinguishing possessions of our city.
> (RCS Archives & Collections, Glasgow Athenaeum Minute Books, Vol. 1, p. 26)

It is surprising that it only took them ten months, but, by 13 October of that year, the Glasgow Athenaeum was already welcoming members to their temporary premises in the Assembly Rooms on Glasgow's Ingram Street.

Unlike its counterparts south of the border, however, the Glasgow Athenaeum did not consider its remit to be elitist or exclusive. Moses Provan was clear: the Glasgow Athenaeum was for 'all of the community' and it seems that he meant it.

Academy orchestra in the Stevenson Hall, 1970s
(Photo: RCS Archives & Collections)

A collaborative performance of Britten's *A Midsummer Night's Dream* between the Royal Conservatoire of Scotland and Scottish Opera in 2013
(Photo: KK Dundas)

Kurt Weill's American opera *Street Scene*, performed in the New Athenaeum Theatre in 2018, featuring cast from across the Conservatoire and the Junior Conservatoire
(Photo: Robert McFadzean)

2

Education for All

THE PROVISIONAL ATHENAEUM COMMITTEE worked hard throughout 1847 to attract interest and subscribers to their new venture. The minutes of their meetings still survive in the Conservatoire's archives, and they reveal the depth and range of their discussions. After weeks of committees and sub-committees, the founders of the Glasgow Athenaeum eventually returned to Moses Provan's prospectus, finally crystallising around this mission statement:

> To provide mental cultivation, moral improvement and delightful recreation to all classes.

Behind the Victorian wording is an important truth: membership of the Glasgow Athenaeum was open 'to all'.

By February 1847, the Provisional Committee had moved from Steel's Coffee House (a male-only space in practice, if not in policy) to Gardner's Temperance Hotel, which welcomed a more mixed clientele. The shift in venue also brought other changes. Steel's Coffee House was to be found near Argyle Street's junction with Queen Street, which, even in the early Victorian era, was a busy commercial and social thoroughfare. North Hanover Street, where Gardner's Temperance Hotel was situated, was a much quieter prospect. There, discussions could take place without the interruptions of passing traffic and the hubbub of Victorian music halls, theatres, pubs and street sellers. We don't find any women's names in the minutes of the Provisional Athenaeum

Committee meetings, yet their early discussions make it clear that the institution was not intended to be exclusively male. This is partly what is meant by the awkward wording 'to all classes'. When the Glasgow Athenaeum opened its doors in October 1847, it welcomed all who could afford the membership fee of seven shillings and sixpence (the equivalent of around £30 today, or one day's wages of a skilled tradesperson), which bought an annual ladies' ticket, or quarterly gentlemen's ticket. As envisioned by Moses Provan, the facilities included access to social areas: a news room or reading room, a library and a coffee room, and there is nothing to suggest that there was any gender segregation in any of these areas. In fact, quite the opposite was true.

'The Athenaeum' elegantly carved in blond sandstone
above the front door
(Photo: Robert McFadzean)

Having found accommodation in the Assembly Rooms and arranged a programme of classes and suitable lecturers for the opening of the Glasgow Athenaeum, one final task fell to the

Provisional Athenaeum Committee: the arrangements for a formal opening ceremony. Chief among their concerns was the selection of presiding officer; one with sufficient clout to draw not only new members, but also the attention of the press. They made a list in order of preference:

    1. Lord Morpeth
    2. Charles Dickens, Esq
    3. B Disraeli, Esq
    4. Sergeant Falfound
    5. Mr Macaulay
    6. Lord John Manners
    7. Mr Douglas Jerrold
    8. Mr Carlyle
    (RCS Archives & Collections,
    Glasgow Athenaeum Minute Books, Vol. 1, p79)

Despite the fact that the much-vaunted reformist and anti-bigotry campaigner Lord Morpeth was either unavailable or unapproachable, the Provisional Committee didn't have to travel too far down their list. A few years earlier, Charles Dickens had formally opened the Manchester Athenaeum, and his growing reputation as a writer and social commentator made him an obvious choice for Chair. At this time, he was at the height of his literary powers having already published some of his most enduring works such as *Oliver Twist* (1837) and *Nicholas Nickleby* (1838). *Dombey and Son* (1846) had recently been published, but perhaps his greatest works were still ahead of him: *David Copperfield* (1849) was in train, but *A Tale of Two Cities* (1859) and *Great Expectations* (1860) were not yet thought of.

The 'Opening Soirée' of the Glasgow Athenaeum took place on 28 December 1847 in the City Halls, and remarkably Dickens's speech on that occasion still survives. In it, he singles out for comment the equality of access that the Athenaeum proffered:

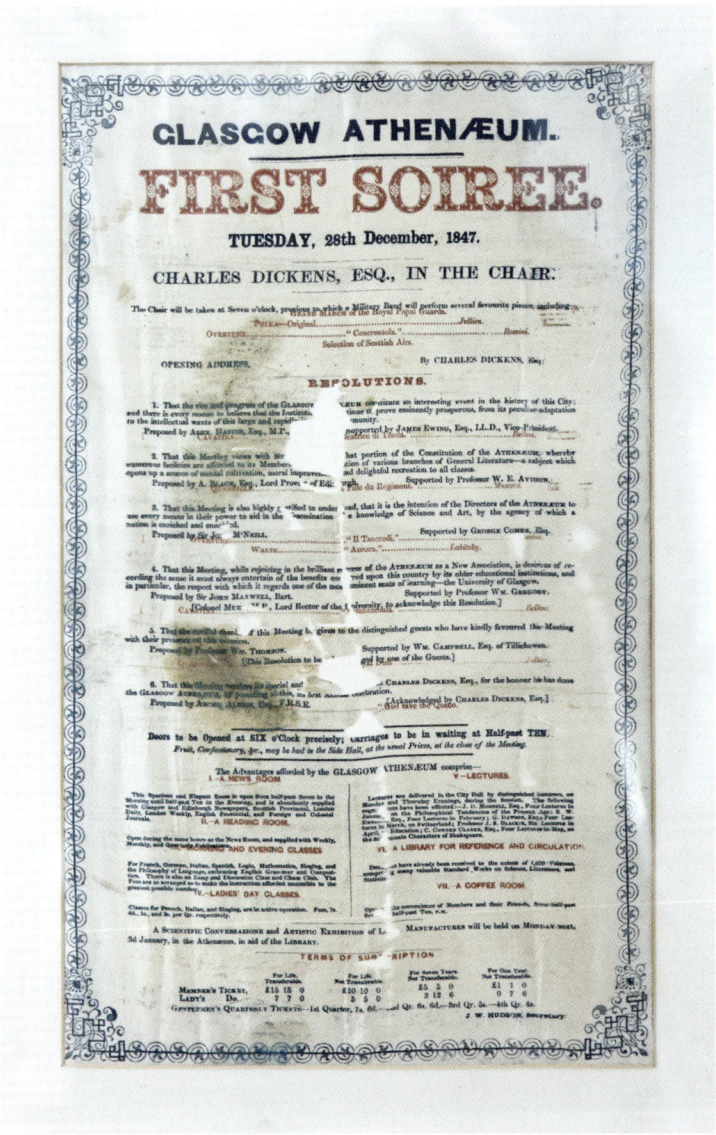

This delicate silk textile commemorating the Glasgow Athenaeum First Soirée, 28 December 1847, hangs in the Principal's Office to this day
(Photo: KK Dundas)

I am happy to know that in the Glasgow Athenaeum there is a peculiar bond of union between the institution and the fairest part of creation. I understand that the necessary addition to the small library of books being difficult and expensive to make, the ladies have generally resolved to hold a fancy bazaar, and to devote the proceeds to this admirable purpose; and I learn with no less pleasure that her Majesty the Queen, in a graceful and womanly sense of the excellence of this design, has consented that the bazaar shall be held under her royal patronage. I can only say, that if you do not find something very noble in your books after this, you are much duller students than I take you to be. The ladies – the single ladies, at least – however disinterested I know they are by sex and nature, will, I hope, resolve to have some of the advantages of these books, by never marrying any but members of the Athenaeum. It seems to me it ought to be the pleasantest library in the world.

(Dickens' Speech, 28 December 1847)

Precisely what Dickens means by 'a peculiar bond of union' is an open question, and probably best left to the imagination, but the fundamental point shines through the innuendo. Women would

The Glasgow Athenaeum 'Book of Strangers', signed by Charles Dickens at the opening soirée, 1847
(Photo: KK Dundas)

The dining room in the Old Athenaeum, c.1910
(Photo: RCS Archives & Collections)

attend the same lectures as men, read the same newspapers in the same reading room and listen to the same concerts. Perhaps in the Victorian era that would have been considered peculiar; it was certainly forward-thinking, and a very welcome foundation stone in our history. It is a sobering fact that the London Athenaeum, still operating as a private members' club today, did not allow women membership until compelled to do so by anti-discrimination legislation. That was in 2002.

In this wording 'to all classes' we also find a wider application. During the first year alone, the Glasgow Athenaeum had welcomed visitors from as far afield as Greenland, Newfoundland, Berlin, Paris, New York and Millport (as recorded in RCS Archives & Collections, Glasgow Athenaeum Book of Strangers). It seems that a spirit of openness and the sharing of knowledge was integral to the founding principles of the institution; what we would now recognise as a commitment to equality, diversity and inclusion was woven into the fabric of the Glasgow Athenaeum from the very beginning, albeit couched within the sensibilities of the Victorian mind.

A piano student in a teaching room in the Old Athenaeum in 1985
(Photo: RCS Archives & Collections)

Rehearsal of a choir and orchestral project at Glasgow Cathedral in 2009
(Photo: KK Dundas)

New Dreams, a collaborative celebration to mark the 400th anniversary of Shakespeare's death, with the Royal Conservatoire of Scotland, The Glasgow School of Art, BBC Scottish Symphony Orchestra and the University of Glasgow in 2016
(Photo: KK Dundas)

Dancer Bryony Robertson poses at Dumfries House for the launch of a partnership between the Royal Conservatoire of Scotland and The Prince's Foundation, 2016
(Photo: KK Dundas)

3

First Steps

ONE OF THE Glasgow Athenaeum's earliest visiting lecturers was the renowned American philosopher and essayist Ralph Waldo Emerson, who had embarked upon a European speaking tour in 1848. His advertised programme included two lectures; one on 'Napoleon, the Man of Action,' and another mysteriously titled 'Domestic Life'. In the end, however, he changed his mind, and the two lectures he actually delivered were entitled 'The Characteristics of the Six New England States' and 'The Genius of the Present Age'. Emerson, a staunch abolitionist, was considered one of the most liberal and enlightened thinkers of his time. His invitation to speak as one of the first guest lecturers for the Glasgow Athenaeum's inaugural session seems significant; it underlines the liberal principles with which the institution wished to be associated.

Large-scale public lectures appear to have been the mainstay of the Athenaeum in its early years. Addresses given around this time were varied and eclectic, including lectures on the 'philosophical principles of the present age,' to 'the subordinate characters of Shakespeare'. These complemented the regular digest of morning and evening classes, which ranged from logic and mathematics to singing, modern languages (French, German, Italian and Spanish) and the philosophy of language (ie English grammar and syntax). There were also essay and discussion classes, as well as a chess club. In all, the directors of the Athenaeum were keen to stress that 'the fees are so arranged as to make the instruction afforded accessible to the greatest possible number' (RCS Archives & Collections, Glasgow Athenaeum Minute Books, Vol. 1). Lectures were given in the City

Hall, while the remainder of the syllabus was catered for in the Athenaeum's own reading room, open from 7:30am until 10:30pm.

1848 was an important year in the social and cultural life of Glasgow. On 27 September, the celebrated Polish pianist and composer Frédéric Chopin gave a recital in the old Merchants' Halls on Hutcheson Street, just a few blocks down from the Glasgow Athenaeum's temporary home in the Assembly Rooms on Ingram Street. According to press reviews at the time, the concert was considered to have been a success; Chopin's own view of his Scottish tour was vastly different. In his personal diaries, now published, he noted how frustrated and depressed he was at what he saw as the excessive attentions of elderly lords and ladies more interested in shooting parties than music; he felt the want of young people to stimulate him. He was similarly scathing about the weather.

Chopin's experiences could have been coloured not just by the outdoor pursuits of dreary Scottish aristocrats, but also by his declining health. Although suffering from the late stages of tuberculosis, he was apparently compelled to continue to perform for financial reasons. He died the following year, and although he continued to give recitals almost until the end of his life, his ability to perform was increasingly curtailed. His last ever performance in the Guildhall, London, is widely agreed to have been a pale reflection of the virtuoso's previous heights.

Yet for all this, Chopin's tour of Scotland, and performances in Glasgow in particular, were a watershed moment for the city. The increased visibility of Glasgow on the world stage led the Athenaeum to become a prominent locus for the arts and new thinking in the city, in addition to attracting literary lectures from some of the leading authors of the day. William Makepeace Thackeray delivered a lecture on 'The Four Georges' in November 1856 (part of a series he later published) and in 1870 Anthony Trollope spoke on 'Prose Fiction as a Rational Amusement'. Lectures varied from light subjects to profound political and constitutional matters.

The first woman to be invited to speak to the members of

the Athenaeum was the celebrated feminist and women's rights advocate Emily Faithfull. Her lecture on 'The Vexed Question' (promoting the enfranchisement of women) in 1871 foreshadowed an important societal shift which was then gaining momentum, and with which the Glasgow Athenaeum (by giving her a platform) was to become associated.

Emily Faithfull was an English equal rights activist and publisher, a member of the Society for Promoting the Employment of Women and co-founder of the Women's Printing Society. In 1860, Faithfull had established the Victoria Press as a vehicle for allowing more women to find employment in the publishing business. Her success and reputation for excellence was such that she was appointed Printer and Publisher in Ordinary to Queen Victoria.

The Victoria Press appears to have specialised in the publication of pamphlets and periodicals, such as the *English Women's Journal* and the eponymous *Victoria Magazine*. These feminist works were important arenas for debate on the furtherance of equal rights and the cause of universal suffrage. Her invitation to travel from London to Glasgow to speak to the members of the Glasgow Athenaeum underlines its commitment to freedom of debate and access for all, and represents an important departure from the social orthodoxy of the time.

Faithfull was invited to speak again in December 1873, and her popularity (the City Hall was full on both occasions) led to the Athenaeum inviting more women to lecture. These included Lydia Becker, discussing the portrayal of female characters in the works of Sir Walter Scott, and Millicent Garrett Fawcett (later to gain fame as a leading suffragette and feminist union leader) on 'Some Female Characters of George Eliot'.

It would be wrong to claim that the Glasgow Athenaeum, in aligning itself with abolitionists and suffragettes, was an institution unsullied by the dreadful proceeds of slavery and which held itself aloof from the prevailing preconceptions and misconceptions of Victorian sociopolitics. The rapid industrialisation of Glasgow

McLennan Arch at the west entrance to Glasgow Green, the old front door to the Assembly Rooms, moved from Ingram Street when the building was demolished in the 1880s. It had moved several times around the city before being relocated here in 1991
(Photo: Robert McFadzean)

in the 18th and 19th centuries saw a vast influx of wealth from human trafficking and slavery via trade in tobacco, sugar and textiles. No institution of the age was unblemished by association, however the Glasgow Athenaeum does appear to have been an establishment which prided itself on freedom of debate. In its choice of speakers and subject matter, the organisers showed no fear in tackling the thornier issues of the day. It underscores Moses Provan's dictum, that education and the Glasgow Athenaeum were, and are, 'for all'.

Conductor Sir Donald Runnicles accompanies Annush Hovhannisyan in the Stevenson Hall, 2012
(Photo: KK Dundas)

A production of *Owen Wingrave* in the New Athenaeum Theatre, 2016
(Photo: KK Dundas)

A student tests out the new stage flying technology in the New Athenaeum Theatre in 2009
(Photo: KK Dundas)

4

Moving

ALTHOUGH THE GLASGOW ATHENAEUM had occupied the Assembly Rooms for over 30 years, this was to prove only a temporary home. It had been steadily increasing its share of interest in the building, presumably hoping to succeed to outright proprietorship, since the prearranged 'Tontine System' of ownership would allow the last tenant standing to win ownership of the entire building. The city planners had other ideas.

In the 1880s, Glasgow's General Post Office on George Square was running out of space and needed to expand. Occupying a large portion of the south side of George Square, the only space available was behind, into the Assembly Rooms. They were scheduled for demolition. The directors of the Athenaeum, faced with this dilemma, transformed it into an opportunity. Although the Assembly Rooms had been extensively refitted to accommodate the needs and activities of the Athenaeum, the results had always been imperfect. The 1880s saw an opportunity to create a new, custom-built club and land was procured in old St George's Place (now Nelson Mandela Place) for the purpose.

The new building was formally opened by the eminent philanthropist and politician John Crichton-Stuart, third Marquis of Bute, on Wednesday 25 January 1888. The whole venture cost £26,000 (over £2,000,000 in today's terms), and despite the fact that it provided nearly three times the accommodation afforded by the Assembly Rooms, the space was soon found wanting:

From the first day on which the building was opened it

was evident that a new era had been entered upon. The number of members and students increased by leaps and bounds, and the progress was so often referred to in the newspapers and elsewhere as 'phenomenal,' that by-and-bye some ingenuity was demanded to invent a new word to describe the Institution's rapid progression [...] It very soon became apparent that, large as the new building was, it was yet quite inadequate to meet the growing development which had so suddenly taken place, and the Directors felt themselves placed in a dilemma. (Lauder, *Athenaeum*, p. 120)

A further extension was budgeted for and completed on Buchanan Street, which can still be recognised by its sandstone façade as the 'Old Athenaeum Building'. It was formally opened on 17 March 1893 at the cost of a further £40,000 (nearly £3,500,000 in today's money). This extension provided much needed performance space, including a public theatre and a separate upstairs recital hall, necessitated by perhaps the most seismic shift yet within the institution.

Exterior of the 'new' Buchanan Street building showing the extension entrance to the right c.1975
(Photo: RCS Archives & Collections)

Traditional musician Hannah Rarity (centre) takes to the Celtic Connections stage in 2014 (Photo: KK Dundas)

Oskar McCarthy performs in *Eight Songs for a Mad King*, in Cottiers Theatre in 2020, one of the last RCS performances before the COVID-19 national lockdown
(Photo: Robert McFadzean)

Guitarist Sean Shibe pictured in a rehearsal in 2009
(Photo: KK Dundas)

A co-production of *War and Peace* between RCS and Scottish Opera in 2009
(Photo: KK Dundas)

5

Athenaeum School of Music

MUCH LIKE A character in a long-running soap opera, the Glasgow Athenaeum has, on occasion, had to reinvent itself. The first time this happened was in 1890, in a pivotal breaking of new ground that saw the establishment of the Athenaeum School of Music and its partner, the Athenaeum College of Commerce. The idea had long been in gestation, and the need for a music school in Scotland that could train artists and performers to an international standard was becoming ever more obvious. Glasgow alone had just produced two of Europe's leading contemporary pianists, Eugen d'Albert and Frederic Lamond, both of whom had to move to the continent to pursue their careers.

Eugen d'Albert was born in Glasgow in April 1864, the son of a former ballet master at the King's Theatre in London's Covent Garden. Among his ancestors, he could count the Italian composers Giuseppe Matteo Alberti and Domenico Alberti, now recognised as one of the most significant voices in the transition from the Baroque to Classical periods. Although at a young age d'Albert received musical training from both his father and the National Training School for Music in London (later to become the Royal College of Music), his international acclaim was only achieved after he won the Mendelssohn Scholarship which enabled him to move to Vienna. There he would meet the now elderly international superstar Franz Liszt, and under his tutelage (among others) d'Albert would go on to become one of the most famous

A meeting of the Board of Governors to mark the 50th anniversary
of the Glasgow Athenaeum, 1897
(Photo: RCS Archives & Collections)

pianists of his generation and a prolific composer in his own right.

Frederic Lamond's story follows a similar trajectory. Lamond was born in Glasgow in January 1868, and similarly moved to Europe at a young age to pursue his passion for classical piano, studying in Frankfurt under the familiar names Hans von Bülow, Clara Schumann and, of course, Franz Liszt. Lamond studied with Liszt in the 1880s and would sometimes travel with the maestro as he gave masterclasses around the continent. Perhaps a lesser-known name today than d'Albert, and unfairly so, Lamond was

Frederic Lamond bronze bust by Alexander Proudfoot located outside one of the Conservatoire's recital rooms
(Photo: Robert McFadzean)

also one of the most celebrated performers of his generation, and often lauded in his day as the definitive exponent of Beethoven's works for piano. A bust of him by Glasgow School of Art graduate Alexander Proudfoot looms outside one of the Conservatoire's recital rooms to this day.

Having felt the lack of a school of sufficient standard in Scotland to train such emerging international talent, yet another Scot who studied in Europe would step up to fill the breach: Allan Macbeth. Born in Greenock in 1856, considerably less is known about Macbeth's career than those of d'Albert and Lamond, however, we do know that he received his musical training in the highly prestigious Leipzig Conservatorium. By 1880, Macbeth was conducting the Glasgow Choral Union, as well as composing and arranging his own music.

It is against this backdrop that the Glasgow Athenaeum School of Music was formally launched in 1890, with Allan Macbeth as its founding principal. A new venture, it was Macbeth's wish to recreate a European conservatoire style of instruction in Scotland, where professional musicians, teachers and creatives could be trained to the same standard as those coming out of the more well-known German, Austrian, Russian, Italian and French schools of the time. A tall order, but one which Macbeth appears to have met with boundless energy and vision.

The trend seems to have been international; the Royal College of

Music was founded in London a few years earlier in 1882, and the Moscow Imperial Conservatory (now Moscow State Tchaikovsky Conservatory) was founded a few years before that in 1866. The following year (1867), the Franz Schubert Conservatory, Vienna's oldest private music school, was opened, and – not long after the opening of the Athenaeum School of Music in Glasgow – La Schola Cantorum was established in Paris in 1894.

As with so many similar ventures, their success or failure rested largely on the characters and wills of the individuals who created them, and it was one of Macbeth's strengths that he was able to bring together a unique pool of talent from across the globe to establish his school. Early appointees included the brothers Julius and HAL Seligmann, originally from Hamburg; Albert Rieu, head-hunted from the Paris Conservatoire; Golan E Hoole, who would go on to become the principal of the Conservatory at the College – now University – of Regina, Canada; and the famous Glasgow impresario, composer and conductor J Michael Diack, founder of the Glasgow Bach Choir.

Despite an already impressive cast, even more exalted names were to follow.

PROFILE: Henri Verbrugghen

Henri Verbrugghen
(Photo: RCS Archives & Collections)

Henri Verbrugghen was born in Brussels in August 1873 and was a prize-winning student of the famed violin teachers Jenö Hubay and

Eugène-Auguste Ysaÿe at the Brussels Conservatorium. A stellar career followed his graduation more or less immediately, including leading the Scottish Orchestra (forerunner of the Royal Scottish National Orchestra) and giving the UK première of Sibelius' *Violin Concerto in D-Minor*.

In 1904, Verbrugghen was invited to join the professors at the Glasgow Athenaeum School of Music, becoming the de facto head of strings. It was to be the springboard that launched his teaching career, as in 1915 he was invited to become the founding principal of the Sydney Conservatorium – an invitation he accepted. While there, he almost accidentally founded the Sydney Symphony Orchestra, and his contribution to Australian musical life is well commemorated. There is a Verbrugghen Street in Canberra, Australia's capital, and the main concert hall of the Sydney Conservatorium is called the Verbrugghen Hall.

In addition to possessing legendary whiskers, Verbrugghen appears to have been a performer with ants in his pants. By 1922 he found himself the resident conductor of the Minneapolis Symphony Orchestra, and in 1933 he was appointed chair of the department of music at Carleton College, Northfield, Minnesota.

It all began for him in Glasgow, where his reputation not only as a virtuoso violinist but as an educator and leader of considerable skill was established. As yet, there is no Verbrugghen Street in Glasgow.

PROFILE: Emma Ritter-Bondy

Emma Ritter-Bondy
(Photo: John Ritter)

Even before Verbrugghen, in the very early days of the Athenaeum School of Music, came an arguably more significant appointment. In 1891, the name 'Madame Ritter-Bondy' appears among the list of professors of the school, a lone female figure among a sea of male names.

Emma Ritter-Bondy was born in Graz, in what is now Austria, in January 1838 and studied piano at the Vienna Conservatory.

After a much-fêted performance career touring modern-day Austria and Germany, she settled into a teaching career at the Königlichen Gymnasium zu Coblenz, today's Görres-Gymnasium in Koblenz. Although Ritter-Bondy's name appears in 1891 as professor of piano at the Athenaeum School of Music, the Conservatoire's archives hold no definitive record of her actually teaching students until the following year. That aside, the early date of this appointment is significant. The title of 'professor' was an elevated one, above the other teaching staff and intended to indicate a higher status. This makes Emma Ritter-Bondy the first woman to be appointed a professor in an educational institution in the United Kingdom.

By 1890, the Glasgow Athenaeum School of Music had moved away from the private members' club model and had grown into what one would now class as a further education establishment, able to appoint professors much like colleges and academies throughout the country offering sub-degree level instruction. Edith Morley is widely credited as the first woman in the UK to have been appointed a professor in the English Literature department of the University of Reading in 1908, and Margaret Fairlie is often seen as the first woman in Scotland to enjoy the same status as Chair of Gynaecology at what is now the University of Dundee in 1940. Emma Ritter-Bondy significantly predates both.

Her career in education in Glasgow was cut short by her death in June 1894. Following her husband's death in 1879, as a single mother of two, she had spent 15 years travelling in Europe, supporting her children through her pianistic craft. Both of her children became celebrated musicians in their own right, her daughter Ida as a piano accompanist, and her son Camillo as a violinist, composer and teacher, who followed in his mother's footsteps by teaching at the Glasgow Athenaeum School of Music. Emma Ritter-Bondy's legacy is one of tenacity and perseverance against an undoubtedly patriarchal system, over which she ultimately triumphed.

Cellist Jalayne Mitchell relaxes during a creative performance on the New Athenaeum Theatre stage in 2019
(Photo: Robert McFadzean)

Junior Conservatoire of Music rehearse in the Stevenson Hall
(Photo: Robert McFadzean)

A production student puts the final touches to a 15 foot champagne bottle used in a production of *Die Fledermaus* in 2017
(Photo: Julie Howden)

Lauren Macdonald, first female BMus Jazz drummer to study at RCS, performs in 2015
(Photo: KK Dundas)

6

Active Society for the Propagation of Contemporary Music

DESPITE THE VAGUELY botanical associations of its name, the Active Society (for short) was the brainchild of Glasgow Athenaeum and Edinburgh University alumnus, Erik Chisholm. It was an ambitious venture, intended to promote the world's best contemporary classical music and musicians, bringing them together in Glasgow.

Erik William Chisholm was born in Glasgow in January 1904. He studied piano and composition under Philip Halstead at the Athenaeum School of Music, before completing a PhD under musicologist Sir Donald Francis Tovey at Edinburgh University. Chisholm was a keen proponent of traditional Scottish music in the wider performing arts; he co-founded the Celtic Ballet with Margaret Morris (wife of the Scottish Colourist JD Fergusson) and was the first composer to incorporate the Scottish idiom, and particularly the tropes and motifs found in traditional Gaelic folk music, into classical pieces. For instance, his first piano concerto, an orchestral work in four movements completed while he was still a student, incorporates many of the evolutions and figures associated with highland bagpipe music (*ceòl mòr*), which led to it becoming known as the *Piobaireachd Concerto*.

Early in his career, alongside friends and fellow composers Francis George Scott and Pat Shannon, Chisholm founded the Active Society which built on Glasgow's burgeoning reputation as a venue for classical and contemporary music performance. The Active Society brought internationally renowned composers

such as Béla Bartók, Paul Hindemith, Arnold Bax, William Walton and Kaikhosru Sorabji to Glasgow to conduct and perform their own works, in productions which were often UK, and occasionally world, premières. One of the many jewels of the Erik Chisholm Archive held by the RCS is a score dated November 1930 and autographed by the composer Hindemith, which thanks Chisholm for a 'beautiful performance in Glasgow'. The occasion alluded to was a performance of Hindemith's 'Wir Bauen Eine Stadt' ('We Build a Town'), a choral work written earlier that year and given its UK première by our own junior choir alongside the Junior Orpheus Choir. Hindemith also performed his own viola sonata, with Chisholm at the piano, in the same concert.

The Active Society held some of its concerts in the Stevenson Hall, a new addition to the Buchanan Street building. Performance venues such as the Athenaeum Theatre and the Stevenson Hall were the principal asset of this new building, when compared with the previous facilities on Ingram Street. (The Stevenson Hall is named in honour of Sir Daniel Macaulay Stevenson, a former Lord Provost of the City of Glasgow and generous benefactor to the institution.) It takes an effort of will to imagine the Active Society's performance of William Walton's 'Façade' which saw the lyrics delivered via a megaphone poked through a hole in a sheet at the back of the stage.

The aims of the Active Society were very closely aligned with those of Chisholm's alma mater, the Glasgow Athenaeum School of Music. Where Allan Macbeth looked to international talent to establish his conservatoire, Chisholm did the same when planning his concerts. Such decisions speak to the internationality of music;

a universal language which carries meaning across borders and political divides. Despite significant patronage and considerable talent, The Active Society proved financially unviable and only managed to sustain itself for seven years. Not long after it folded, Chisholm accepted a position as Director of the Music College at the University of Cape Town, South Africa, where his pacifism, vegetarianism and anti-apartheid ethics ensured that his politics drew as much attention as his musicianship. On one famous occasion, he staged a protest to oppose the suggestion that trees were to be cut down on the University campus, refusing to play the organ at that year's graduation ceremony unless the plan was abandoned. Naturally, he won.

Erik Chisholm
(Photo: RCS Archives & Collections)

Chisholm's was a precocious talent. He studied at the Athenaeum School of Music at a very young age, graduating top of his class. His gifts and energy were exactly those that Allan Macbeth had envisioned his new conservatoire serving, equipping graduates with the skills necessary to make it in the world of professional classical music making.

Students, staff and alumni of the Royal Conservatoire of Scotland perform at Buckingham Palace, 2019
(Photo: Ian Watt)

Violinists Wen Wang and Gongbo Jiang perform on the rooftop of Gleneagles to mark a new partnership with the Royal Conservatoire of Scotland
(Photo: KK Dundas)

7

Playing On

ALTHOUGH BOTH THE First and Second World Wars brought the nation to a halt in many ways, there was still music to be had. An air raid shelter was installed in the basement of the building (which inevitably played host to instruments more often than people), and the business of teaching and performance continued among both those who hadn't been called up to serve in the war effort, and also by students and staff drafted into ENSA, the Entertainments National Service Association. During this time, word reached Glasgow that the famous Finnish composer Jean Sibelius was in financial straits. It was well-known that Sibelius liked to live a life of luxury, with a rich diet of symphonies and tone poems complemented by lobster and champagne. It proved unsustainable, both financially and medically.

The Choral and Orchestral Union of Glasgow, long associated with the school and sharing many of its personnel, decided to take action. A hat was almost literally passed around to raise money to aid the composer, and the healthy sum of £233 13s 5d (around £8,500 in today's money) was raised. Unfortunately for Sibelius, however, the Union had forgotten to take into account the regulations governing the movement of money during this time; in the immediate post-war period the country was rebuilding, both literally and fiscally, and such large sums were prohibited from leaving the country.

After corresponding directly with Sibelius (the letters still survive in the Conservatoire's archives), it was agreed that the

William Gillies Whittaker conducting the concerto class in the Stevenson Hall, c.1930
(Photo: RCS Archives & Collections)

money would be invested in the form of a prize in the name of the composer himself. The Sibelius Prize is still awarded at the end of every year to two undergraduate students for the best essays on a 20th or 21st century subject. Fortunately for Sibelius himself, his own fortunes also recovered after the war, making the prize a symbol of the resilience of the arts through times of privation. That, and a possibly tongue-in-cheek memorial to excess.

Since its foundation, the music school has offered training in all the traditional orchestral sections (strings, woodwind, brass, keyboard and percussion), as well as singing, the rudiments of music (musical notation classes) and harmony and counterpoint. Innovation continued to drive the school to a greater clarity of focus, in particular with formal training in composition established under composer and teacher Frank Spedding in 1960, the institution of a formal Junior Academy Orchestra under the viola player James Durrant in 1964, and the formation of an official brass department under the horn player Maurice Temple in 1986. Later, the remit expanded to include music teacher training, opera classes and traditional Scottish music (including Scots Gaelic and bagpipe repertoire) – the UK's only Bachelor of Music degree dedicated to traditional and folk music.

Musical training through the mid to late 20th century followed a conventional mode, wherein students were encouraged to practice their classical technique to the exclusion of all other forms. Occasionally, this could prove controversial, as in the case of Jack Bruce, who won a scholarship to study 'cello and composition in 1958. When his teachers discovered that he was playing in Jim McHarg's Scotsville Jazzband to support himself through his studies, they issued him with an ultimatum: stop playing jazz (as it would ruin his technique), or face being expelled. Bruce found a third way and quit. It was to be the making of his career, as he would go on to become one of the most celebrated and important Rock bassists of all time, both in the band Cream (with Eric Clapton and Ginger Baker) and as a solo performer.

It took a long time for the conventional wisdom to come around to Jack Bruce's point of view, but finally, in 2009, a degree in Jazz joined the curriculum.

Early teaching in the Junior Academy including tablecloth pianos, c.1940
(Photo: RCS Archives & Collections)

SPOTLIGHT: Tommy Smith

(Photo: Aldo Ferraldo)

With the support of Sean Connery's Scottish International Education Trust, I left Scotland in a mist to begin my study of jazz at Berklee College of Music in Boston, USA, aged 16, and my difficult journey began. After 16 months of jazz education, I was invited to tour the world, performing concerts and presenting jazz educational workshops with renowned vibist and educator Gary Burton, Vice President of Berklee College of Music; I was only 18. The countries I experienced and taught jazz improvisation in over the next three decades were France, Holland, Russia, Kazakhstan, USA, Yemen, Ireland, Sweden, Uzbekistan, Czech Republic, Turkey, Iceland, Finland, Switzerland, England, Romania, China, India, Pakistan, Canada, Nicaragua and Norway.

After being signed to the world-renowned record label Blue Note in 1988 for a lucrative four-album deal, living in Paris and touring the world, I decided to come home to Edinburgh in 1993, a decade after I left. I saw a lack of jazz infrastructure, leadership, and opportunity in Scotland compared to all the countries I had taught and performed in.

In 1993, I began teaching and developing improvisation at Napier University, for only 24 days each year. In 1994, I moved my focus to Strathclyde University, but again for only 24 days annually. In 1995, I established the National Jazz Institute focused on weekends, again 24 days annually. The Alumni from NJI include: Mario Caribe, Paul Towndrow, Stephen Duffy, Konrad Wiszniewski, Tom MacNiven and Graeme Scott. That year, I also founded the Scottish National Jazz Orchestra, which is now over a quarter of a century old.

From 2001, I pleaded the case for a full-time Jazz course in Scotland. I wrote to the First Minister and Head of the Scottish Executive Jack McConnell, the Deputy First Minister and Minister for Justice Jim Wallace, and the Minister for Education and Young People Cathy Jamieson. I was also advised to meet with the Minister for Tourism, Culture and Sport Mike Watson and the Minister for Enterprise, Transport and Lifelong Learning Iain Gray, which I did. All replied courteously; none could do anything. Then I met executives at the Scottish Higher Education Funding Council accompanied by Heriot-Watt University secretary Peter Wilson and Roger Spence from Assembly Direct; both Roger and Peter were keen to establish a new school built from the ground up at Heriot-Watt, and at the time were even prepared to construct a new building dedicated to jazz. I can still imagine it now.

Fundamentally, no Scottish Minister nor Scottish Higher Education

Tommy pictured here as he prepares to conduct the Jazz Orchestra in their Miles Ahead concert with Laura Jurd in 2017
(Photo: Julie Howden)

Funding Council could make any move or direct any educational body to focus on jazz. All my time up to this point had been wasted, and I learned only one dark thing; each educational institution could make its own mind up.

Jazz is widely recognised as one of the most important musical genres of the 21st century. Still, when jazz education proliferated throughout Europe in the 1960s, Scotland resisted the temptation to add full-time Jazz courses to its curriculums. Why?

In North America, Jazz had been successfully taught since 1945 at Berklee. They have approximately 5,000 students from 98 countries, primarily Korea, Canada, Japan, Mexico and Italy (30% female, 28% international, 9% African American, 12% Hispanic, 24,427 online students, three record labels, five internet radio channels, 20 summer programmes, $35,000,000 annual scholarship fund, 231 alumni Grammy Awards). In Europe, Jazz had been taught for 50 years throughout Sweden, Denmark, Germany, Italy, Norway, Finland, Portugal, France, Spain, Holland, Ireland, Austria, Poland, Wales and England. How many full-time collegiate Jazz courses are there in the world? Over 500. In Scotland, there were none.

In 2002, I met with the new principal of the Royal Scottish Academy of Music and Drama, John Wallace, who I knew adored jazz. We had played some Miles Davis together when I was a guest with the London Symphonia years back, and I thought he might be able to change the tide and prejudice against improvised music.

Peter Wilson, from Heriot-Watt had already budgeted what we needed, and he and I both knew it could work. Still, we discovered that certain pig-headed people in Scottish education did not wish to see jazz taught or mooted in the corridors of the classical establishment. A few weeks after our meeting in Glasgow, John Wallace apologised and said, 'sorry, we're not ready yet for jazz'. Instinctively, I knew the opposition came from the RSAMD board, not Wallace. After the disappointment, I met with the Principals of Napier University and Stevenson College in Edinburgh. Again, a dead-end street. It was time to be very patient, focus on other things, and wait for Scotland to catch up with the rest of the world and lose their fear of free music; African-American music.

After establishing my record company Spartacus Records, in 2000, so titled as I was free from any corporate leadership, I established my youth jazz orchestra in 2002. An elite ensemble, where we invited the most talented of Scotland's young jazz musicians to be part of something you couldn't pay to be part of; only talent was your ticket in. A few years later, I co-founded the Scottish Jazz Federation and personally presented four big ideas: a full-time Jazz course, a youth Jazz competition, Scottish Jazz Awards and regional youth Jazz Orchestras.

In 2007, the Scottish Jazz Federation established the Young Scottish Jazz Musician of the Year, and that same year I delivered a speech to the Scottish Government about the need for jazz education in Scotland. In 2008 the Scottish Jazz Federation established the Scottish Jazz Awards.

Then right out of the blue, like a dream, I received a telephone call: 'We'd like you to head up a full-time jazz course at the RSAMD'. John Wallace then drove to my house and we talked through what the plan for jazz would be. The rest is history.

Tommy Smith
Award-winning saxophonist and educator. Founder of the Scottish National Jazz Orchestra and the Tommy Smith Youth Jazz Orchestra.

Nicola Benedetti, Patron of RCS Junior Conservatoire of Music, gives a masterclass in the Ledger Recital Room in 2016
(Photo: Julie Howden)

SPOTLIGHT: Pamella Dow

Pamella Dow in action, teaching one of her Saturday morning Junior Conservatoire percussion classes in 2018
(Photo: Robert McFadzean)

I used to go to the beautiful Caird Hall in Dundee to hear the Scottish National Orchestra play, and I was absolutely captivated by Leslie Newland on the timpani; I just thought this was the bee's knees. After seeing him, I asked my teachers at Dundee's Morgan Academy if I could have lessons on percussion, and I started doing that.

After school, I wanted to see how far I could take it so I got in touch with the Royal Scottish Academy of Music. I auditioned and I got in, but they told me I could only take timpani as a second study; I had to do first study piano. They had never had a first study timpanist or percussionist. I thought: I'm not a pianist, I don't want to be a pianist – it's not what I wanted to study. I wanted to be a percussionist, and I was disappointed they didn't have a first study course, so I turned them down and gave them my reasons.

In a very short space of time, I don't think it was even one week, I got a phone call inviting me to come back to Glasgow for a chat. They explained again that they had never taught timpani and percussion as a first study, and would I reconsider taking it as a second study? There were some other students doing timpani but they were all taking it as a second study. But that wasn't my dream. I told them that the world would stop turning if we only did things the same way because they had always been done that way. I was only a teenager!

Two days later they came around to my way of thinking, and they offered me first study timpani. That was in 1961.

I was not very popular to start with. The students who were already there taking timpani and percussion as second study were a little resentful that I had stuck to my guns and insisted on taking it as a first study. But that was just to start with and things settled down. The icing on the cake was that Leslie Newland was invited to become my teacher, and we got on like a house on fire.

Pamella Dow, Timpani and Percussion, 1964
Founder member of the BBC Training Orchestra before joining the Royal Scottish National Orchestra as Principal Percussionist.

8

Making a Drama

THE FIRST DRAMA classes at the Glasgow Athenaeum were held in 1886 under the direction of Walter Baynham, author of *The Glasgow Stage*. These early performances were held under the umbrella of the Glasgow Athenaeum Dramatic Club, and although generally favourably reviewed, seem to have been largely in the realms of amateur dramatics. There was always a Shakespeare play in gestation or on stage, and contemporary pieces tended to be avoided. The quality of performances was doubtless variable: one less than sympathetic reporter deigned to suggest that the most dramatic occurrence in the institution came to pass when a cow, having loosed its bonds on Buchanan Street, found its way into the Glasgow Athenaeum and joined the queue at the ticket office. Enough said.

In addition to classes on elocution, deportment and acting for the stage, the Athenaeum Dramatic Club also held celebratory dinners for some of the leading theatrical talents of the day. One of the most famous of these was the supper held for Henry Irving, the first actor to receive a knighthood for services to drama. Irving was a much-lauded talent; a celebratory dinner was held for him in St James Hall in Glasgow in 1883, and further dinners were held in his honour throughout the 1890s. Irving attended the Glasgow Athenaeum Dinner in 1891, accompanied by his manager, Bram Stoker. The most popular entertainment in town at the time was Buffalo Bill's 'Wild West Show,' so Colonel William Cody (aka

Buffalo Bill) also found himself in attendance. The menu from the dinner still survives in the Conservatoire's archives, showing that delicacies such as 'turkey and tongue' and a 'fricassée of tripe' were among the dishes enjoyed.

It is often reported that Irving was the inspiration behind Bram Stoker's iconic character, Dracula, and the resemblance isn't hard to spot. The gossip of the acting world reported that Irving could be a hard task master, often inspiring fear and dread in those who worked for and with him. There is also a theory that Stoker took some inspiration from Glasgow during his 1891 visit with Irving, naming one of his principal characters after the city's Renfield Street.

Signed photograph of Sir Henry Irving
(Photo : RCS Archives & Collections)

Irving wasn't knighted until four years after the dinner that the Athenaeum Dramatic Club held in his honour, so it seems likely that the celebration was simply an excuse for a knees-up. Irving, in common with many actors in the latter half of the Victorian era, was also a Mason; it is possible that this also played a role in the number of celebratory dinners he enjoyed.

Acting and stage performances continued to be an amateur concern in the Glasgow Athenaeum's syllabus into the 20th century, when the popular teacher and dramatist Percival Steeds took over the reins. While elocution remained an important part of the training, the direction of progress was clear and by the

Students at the entrance to the College of Dramatic Art annexe, 1950s
(Photo : RCS Archives & Collections)

middle of the century a more formal course of instruction seemed inevitable.

The need for a formal drama college was underscored by the creation of the Citizens Theatre Company in 1943. The driving force behind its creation was one James Bridie, Scotland's most famous living playwright of the time. The Citizens Theatre initially held their performances in the Athenaeum Theatre before moving to their more familiar home in the old Royal Princess's Theatre in the Gorbals. After this, the lack of theatrical performances on the Athenaeum's stage was keenly felt. Having founded the company, Bridie now turned his attention to training, and began to agitate in

School of Drama students in the Movement Room
on the top floor of the Old Athenaeum, 1957
(Photo : RCS Archives & Collections)

the popular press for the creation of a school specifically devoted to the instruction of professional actors.

Largely as a result of Bridie's advocacy, acting formally entered the institution's teaching syllabus in 1950 with the creation of a discrete but associated College of Dramatic Art. Although Bridie had been the leading voice behind its creation, he did not take up a teaching post, and instead the college opened later that year under founding director Colin Chandler. A graduate of the Royal Academy of Dramatic Art, Chandler had already begun to make a name for himself running the Boltons Theatre in South Kensington, gaining a reputation for programming new and challenging material with an impressive number of transfers to the West End. Fiona Ross, graduate of the drama teaching course (1966–1969) remembered him as:

> Quiet, and understated with a beautiful voice. He had old fashioned matinée idol looks completed by a strand of grey hair always falling across one eye. Always smiling, he was not only encouraging but remarkably tolerant of everyone – students and staff alike. He was called Colin 'Chekhov' due his enduring delight at the works of the Russian playwright.
>
> My abiding memory is of his chain smoking. Of course everyone smoked then, but Colin never used an ashtray or bin. Instead he would line up the fag ends along the window sill or desk. We often wondered what his house looked like.

The very first acting student across the threshold in 1950 was John Cairney.

SPOTLIGHT: John Cairney

(Photo: Stephanie Methven)

We were threatened by being denied admittance by an old fellow in a bowler hat and wing collar holding up a placard saying 'Do Not Enter Here: Theatre is a Place for the Devil! Avoid Temptation!' As soon as I heard that I couldn't wait to get in! I mean, that's what I was after.

    I knew I had suddenly been given a chance and I had to take it. I have never in my life had three happier years, three more profound years. The teachers there were all experienced – all three of them. I mean, you now have this army of assistants at every level to do everything here because all these years have passed and you have learned the need for all this. But we had three teachers.

MAKING A DRAMA

John Cairney and Mary Marquis attend the opening of Speirs Locks Studios in 2012 (Photo: KK Dundas)

We were given experiences we could never have believed, and that's when I first learned about the absolute power the spoken word has when given emphasis. And what was difficult is that I had to learn to speak English as I went along, because the first thing Geoffrey Nethercott told us then was 'from now on you have got to speak English at every opportunity when you go back'.

So I went back to my usual haunts and stood at Parkhead Cross as I had always done and a guy said 'Whit time izzit?'

I thought, here goes!

And the first sentence I ever spoke in English was: 'It's twenty minutes to nine.'

'Whit?!'

'It's twenty minutes to nine by that clock.'

'Whit's up wae you?'

'I am speaking English.'

'Aw godalmighty, yer aff yer heid!'

John Cairney, Diploma in Dramatic Art, 1953
John has worked as actor, recitalist, lecturer, director and theatre consultant, been published as an author and, most recently, exhibited as a painter.

At the same time as the establishment of the senior school, a junior course was created for 10- to 16-year-olds, offering classes on Wednesday and Thursday evenings and Saturday mornings. In the 1950s the course fee was £1 15s (approximately £55 in modern equivalent).

An all-female production of Macbeth takes place
in the Chandler Studio Theatre in 2017
(Photo: Robert McFadzean)

SPOTLIGHT: Jackie Kay

(Photo: Mary McCartney)

I attended the Juniors' drama course between the ages of 12 and 16 (never missing a Wednesday or a Saturday morning) and I can honestly say, no word of a lie, that it changed my life.

It gave me confidence in my imagination, taught me not to have fear when speaking in public, and how to project my voice, taught me how to

Jackie Kay receives her honorary doctorate from RCS in 2010 (Photo: KK Dundas)

improvise, and most importantly made me a whole group of new friends that were different from my school friends and some of those friends I'm still in touch with today. It wasn't just great fun. It opened doors. People often say to me that I should have been an actress when they hear me read my poems, but that's because I went to RSAMD and the things I learnt at that young age have stayed with me for life.

Jackie Kay, Junior Conservatoire alumna
Award-winning poet, playwright and novelist – and Junior Conservatoire alumna – who, from 2016 to 2021, was the Makar, the poet laureate of Scotland.

The music school had incorporated a junior department since its establishment in 1890, although the expectation at that time was very much that the senior students would be directly involved in tutoring their younger counterparts. This would change in 1964 with the appointment of James ('Jimmy') Durrant. Originally contracted as a viola teacher, Durrant later took over conducting the Junior Orchestra; his brilliance as a communicator made him the logical appointment responsible for professionalising the teaching of early years students.

SPOTLIGHT: David Tennant

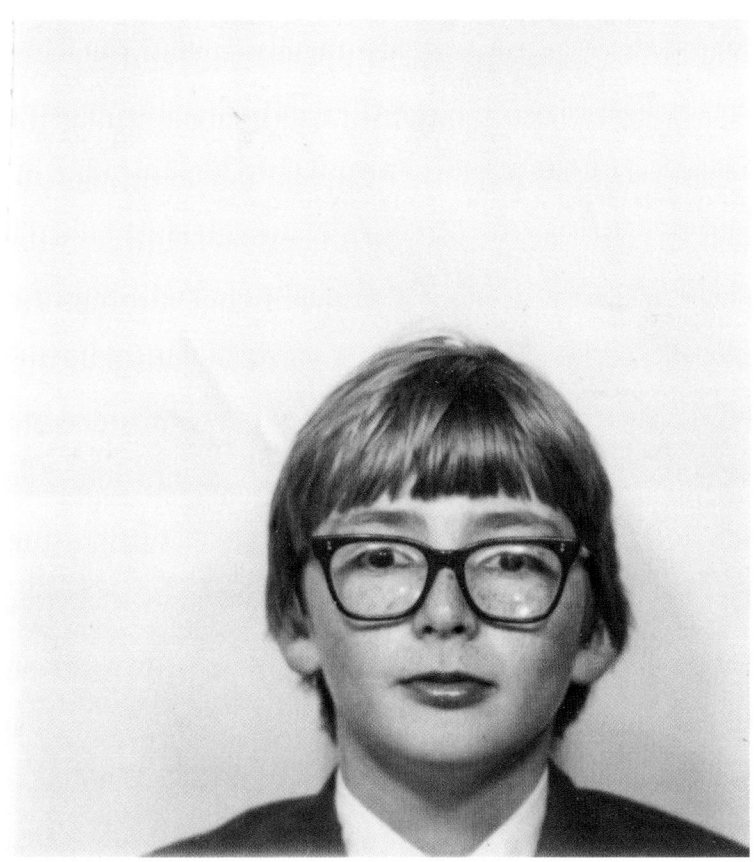

David Tennant's matriculation photograph for the Junior Academy, 1982
(Photo: RCS Archives & Collections)

I came from a background where nobody really knew how you go about becoming an actor. I mean, we were aware that there was the Athenaeum as it was then, so we sniffed around and found out there was a Saturday morning class called the Junior School which you could

David Tennant receives his Honorary Doctorate in 2016
(Photo: KK Dundas)

come to and do classes. I later found out that it was run by the students and it was part of the BA Acting course. At the time, I just thought I was going to a Saturday morning drama club, and I did that every year until I left school and then I came here as a full-time student.

My training was essential because I was very green. I was very young when I came here at 17 – and I was a young 17 – I had little experience except from the Saturday morning classes so my undergraduate training was three years of having a go and practicing. I don't think I would have been able to survive professionally without the training here. From day one, you're mixing with different people, people who are older, have more experience in all sorts of areas of life, but also within acting and within drama and the arts. Just to be amongst this environment was hugely important to me and I grew up very quickly here.

David Tennant in conversation with Andy Dougan on the New Athenaeum stage
(Photo: KK Dundas)

The first time I was in the Chandler Studio, I was in a production of the David Hare play *Fanshen* at the end of my first year. I also did the panto on the Athenaeum stage and I was part of the chorus – I played a Teenage Mutant Ninja Turtle, Raphael, of course.

I was very young when I came to drama school, I was just 17, and my time here was very formative. It was three years of very intensive growing up, experiencing life and I was getting to do what I always wanted to do. It was a huge release coming here straight from school – coming straight from double maths and history and hating every second to here, where it felt like I was released into the world and they were three of the most important years of my life. Those years were hugely informing of who I became and I wouldn't have stood a chance in the professional world without it.

David Tennant, BA Dramatic Studies, 1991
Multi-award-winning theatre, film and television actor. His many and varied roles include BBC's Dr Who and Hamlet in London's West End – he has been described as 'the greatest Hamlet of his generation'. (*The Guardian*)

SPOTLIGHT: James McAvoy

James McAvoy captured in 2015 as he announced the launch of the James McAvoy Scholarship and his position as the Patron of the Junior Conservatoire of Drama
(Photo: KK Dundas)

James McAvoy (left) in *The Beaux Strategem*, 1999
(Photo: KK Dundas)

My training at the RCS benefited me hugely. At RCS, you get three years of doing tons and tons of jobs – by the time you've left, you've worked on 20 different jobs in the first couple of years and you have performed so many times – you just don't get that in the industry.

I'm excited to support the Junior Conservatoire of Drama – it's reaching out to people from disadvantaged backgrounds. I see tons of young people who are so vastly intelligent who, because they have ingrained humility, it gets in the way of them expressing themselves and showing how brilliant they are. Drama especially can help young people break through that and give them the tools to walk into a room, express themselves and show off to the best of their ability.

James McAvoy, BA Acting, 2000
Actor, activist and Scottish global star of stage and screen. Film roles include *X-Men*, *It*, *Split* and *Atonement* and theatre work includes *Cyrano de Bergerac* and *Macbeth*.

School of Drama lecture room being redecorated with posters from Scottish theatres, 1955
(Photo: RCS Archives & Collections)

Initially the College of Dramatic Art had a very small pool of teachers: Colin Chandler taught acting, Geoffrey Nethercott taught voice and Marie Pirie taught movement. They worked out of a red sandstone extension to the Buchanan Street building which had been completed in 1900 and took the footprint of the institution farther around the corner on St George's Place. Ellen Nethercott, alumna (class of 1953) and widow of Geoffrey, recalled the newness of the experience.

> The building had been empty a long time and one shared the space with the rats. As my great aunt used to say you could see them running up the walls on the outside. Time would sometimes have to be spent making the space fit for purpose.
>
> Geoffrey had always been interested in theatre, and when he left the RAF took a job working backstage at the theatre in Exeter. He trained in the Central School of Speech and Drama, after which he moved to Glasgow to take up a post in the College of Dramatic Art. He used phonetics, the placement of the tongue and verse recital in his teaching, and was very much interested in breathing and rib reserve breathing, because we were still on the edge of old-time theatre. There were no microphones, so one had to fill the theatre with one's voice. It was a very good training.

Over the following years the staff expanded, firstly with the movement team. As was the convention in the 1950s, Marie Pirie retired from teaching when she married, and Grace Matchett was appointed her successor. Originally trained in the Ginner-Mawer School of Dance and Drama (which was then in Boscastle, Cornwall) she specialised in ancient Greek theatre and mime. Some years later, she was joined by Peter Lincoln, who had studied under Jacques Leqoc in his world-renowned movement school. It was a school with very strong connections to Glasgow, as remembered by Head of Acting, Joyce Deans:

In 1955, Fay Lees, having completed her first year of drama training in the School of Drama under Colin Chandler, went to Paris to study mime. While studying and working as an actress in Paris, Fay met Jacques Lecoq who had recently returned from eight years in Italy, where he had been choreographing and directing shows, as well as creating the Piccolo Theatre School in Milan with Giorgio Strehler. After his years in Italy, Lecoq felt as if he had been 'squeezed like a lemon,' and now wished to pursue his interest in teaching. In 1956, Fay and Jacques founded what was to become École Jacques Lecoq.

Over the next decade, Colin Chandler continued, through Fay, to maintain a keen interest in the work of the school and in 1967 he sent movement teacher Peter Lincoln to study there. Through Lincoln's movement teaching, the association with École Jacques Lecoq continued to thrive.

In 1965, the South African theatre director Cecil Williams joined the staff. Openly gay, at least in theatrical circles, he cut a debonair figure in the drama corridors. While still in South Africa, Williams had been a vociferous anti-apartheid campaigner, a conviction which ineluctably brought him within the environs of the movement's most famous leader: Nelson Mandela. In his memoirs, Mandela credits Williams for helping him to travel while he was wanted by the authorities; Mandela would pose as Williams' driver so as not to arouse suspicion.

In Glasgow, Williams continued to champion Mandela's anti-apartheid resistance and was an impassioned supporter of the campaign to rename St George's Place in recognition of his friend. His reasoning was twofold; not only was it the home of his drama school, but it was also the address of the South African Consulate, who would have the indignity of having their most high-profile political prisoner's name as part of their address. Sadly, he didn't live to see the name changed; Williams died in 1979 and the street signs weren't changed to 'Nelson Mandela Place' until 1986.

Since these early days, the School of Drama, Dance, Production and Film (as it is now known) has continued to grow both in size and stature, producing a plethora of actors who have become household names. In 1950, there were 23 students in the first year group, including the acting, teaching and technical production arts courses. Today, a typical year group averages around 180 students, incorporating courses in Musical Theatre, Contemporary Performance Practice, Classical and Contemporary Text, Modern Ballet, Performance in British Sign Language and English, Filmmaking and Production Technology and Management.

Coetaneous to the rise in student numbers, the school has also seen an increase in teaching and support staff and, crucially, teaching facilities. One of the most significant additions in recent times has been the establishment of the Centre for Voice in Performance in 2006, with important ramifications for the increased profile of research within the Conservatoire community.

SPOTLIGHT: Ros Steen

(Photo: KK Dundas)

Technology in the modern Conservatoire has overtaken many former ways of doing things. Today, student timetables are electronic. In my student days in the late sixties paper timetables were kept in glass cases, opened by the secretary whose job it was to insert coloured pieces of card into slits in a ladder-like structure and move them around daily, as subjects and rooms changed. Voice, as I recall, was yellow and for me that joyous, uplifting colour is forever associated with the subject.

MAKING A DRAMA

In her book co-written with Frank Spedding, *The First 150 Years*, Grace Matchett chronicled the beginnings of the 'College of Drama' (then RSAMD and now RCS) and recalled early voice teachers whose names are preserved in the titles of their donated prizes – Percival Steeds, Mary Stuart and later Norah Cooper. When I studied the Head of Voice was John Colson, an early advocate for Alexander Technique and Jacqui Crago taught voice, text and phonetics with warm intensity. Voice studies covers a wide spectrum – Technical Voice, Voice Theory, Text work, Radio, Scots Language and Literature, Singing, Verse – and some areas have morphed into newer forms because of technology. Phonetics, for example, is now the digitalised study of Accents and Dialects.

In 1980, the inimitable Jean Moore was appointed Head of Department. The generation of students fortunate enough to be taught by her will remember a forthright approach – very! – combined with the desire to bring out the best in them. During her time a warm relationship was sustained between the RCS and the Royal Shakespeare Company whose Voice Director, the renowned Cicely Berry, visited the school on several occasions. Berry was awarded Fellowship of the Academy in 1987 and it was in the following month that she effected an introduction:

> I saw Nadine George from the Roy Hart Theatre yesterday…
> I gave her your name and she might contact you…

Nadine arrived in 1990 to give her first workshop for students, which I observed. Later I wrote:

> The experience…was unforgettable…she was reaching the parts other voice work wasn't reaching and opening my students in a way I knew should be possible and now was.

The association with Nadine George and her voice work, rooted in the uniqueness of the human voice as the indissoluble expression of each individual, was to have profound and far-reaching impact. As her visits increased she worked with each year group across an expanded portfolio

Nadine George teaches a masterclass with School of Drama students in 2016 (Photo: KK Dundas)

of performance courses. Crucially, she also worked with course staff introducing them to her vocal technique and philosophical approach which resulted in fruitful exchanges.

At the same time the work was being introduced into Scottish Theatre. Joyce McMillan notes in *Theatre in Scotland: A Field of Dreams* that the leading voices of Scottish playwriting which began to emerge during the 1990s helped build a repertoire with a 'huge international reputation'.

It could be said that by 2005, the Voice Department was riding high. Aside from cutting-edge practices in the profession and in training, staff were invited to give papers at international conferences and to publish their work in peer-reviewed journals. International relationships were boosted when colleagues came to observe the work from as far afield as Canada, South Africa, and Australia.

In 2006 restructuring plans were announced which proposed abolishing departments in favour of course-based organisation. Suddenly, the department faced losing autonomy and, without a dedicated department, there was no guarantee voice interests would be safeguarded. A consultative document, *Vocal Vision*, set out strong arguments for keeping the department intact based on proven track record, leading voice practice and research. What emerged was the creation of a Centre for Voice in Performance, which would function internally as a teaching and research unit and externally as a professional practice and research body.

Nadine George Voice Work was formally made the core spoken vocal practice in the School of Drama. RCS became the first conservatoire in the UK to establish NGVW as mainstream practice and the focus of its practice-led research agenda and Nadine George was appointed the RCS's first International Fellow in Voice.

In 2013 the Centre published *Growing Voices – Nadine George Technique: The evolution of its influence in training and performance*. That same year, RCS made its submission to the Research Excellence Framework, the means by which research in British higher education is measured, evaluated and awarded funding. Ratings were given not solely on the quality of the research but its demonstrable impact outside the institution. The research of the Centre for Voice in Performance was chosen as one of two impact case studies and the institution scored well with some 'world-leading' research and a top ranking for 'impact'.

In 2013 Jean Sangster, an alumna of this institution, was appointed my successor. Under her leadership teaching initiatives, professional connections and research have all continued to forge ahead.

The future of the Centre for Voice in Performance seems rosy.

Or perhaps that should be sunshine yellow.

Ros Steen, Diploma of Dramatic Arts, 1972
Scotland's foremost voice specialist, Professor Emerita and former Head of the Centre for Voice in Performance at the Royal Conservatoire of Scotland.

The Wallace Studios – named after previous principal John Wallace – opened in 2010 at Speirs Locks, adding state-of-the-art ballet studios, technical and production facilities and prop and wardrobe stores to the expanding footprint and artistic specialisms of the institution. Designed by Malcolm Fraser Architects, the company behind the redevelopment of Scottish Ballet's headquarters in the city's Southside, the Wallace Studios were created out of derelict, steel-framed warehouses and situated in the north of the city, across the road from Scottish Opera and across the canal from National Theatre of Scotland's first purpose-built hub at Rockvilla. Six years later, the Archives & Collections department moved into a repurposed whisky bond by the canal, next door to Rockvilla.

SPOTLIGHT: Alan Cumming

(Photo: Robert McFadzean)

In the spring of 1982, I took a day off work and travelled to Glasgow to audition for drama school. My mum came with me for moral support. I had to prepare two speeches, one classical, one modern. The modern was from an Irish play I had performed recently with the Carnoustie theatre club, *Lovers* by Brian Friel, and for my classical I chose the 'Look here upon this picture' speech from the chamber scene, Act 3, Scene 4 of *Hamlet*. I could never have imagined that just 11 years later I would be playing Hamlet in London's West End.

    I had no idea what to expect. I had never auditioned for a panel like this before. I had never been to Glasgow before! I had only recently discovered that there was such a thing as the Royal Scottish Academy of Music and Drama, where you could actually go and study acting.

    But the fiancée of my school friend had gone to study drama at the Academy, so I wrote off for a prospectus and suddenly a whole new world of possibility opened up for me.

I read and reread that prospectus like a spy who was about to go undercover, so on the day I finally walked through the Academy doors and was shown around by a lovely student named Margaret-Ann, the place felt almost familiar, like it was the place I was meant to be.

I had discovered I was quite good at it (acting I mean) after doing a play at high school and it was the first time anyone, strangers, had told me I was any good at anything. And so, I stuck with it. At first, I thought people were only complimenting me because I was able to do something they couldn't or would be too afraid to try – and I think the former is in some sense true. Some people just aren't very good at acting and never will be. I suppose they could get some help and become a little less bad, but why bother? It's obviously never going to be their thing, and well, life's too short. Or put it this way: some people are double-jointed or can ride a unicycle, and some people can act.

But after that first high school acting foray, I realized that my school friends and various parents and teachers weren't just giving me false flattery or some version of 'I wish I could do that'. There was something about *me* acting, and the way that I did, that they responded to. I could connect with them when I was onstage. I didn't really understand why at the time, and I suppose one of the reasons I carried on acting was to try to find out. All I knew was I could do something special and I'd never experienced anything like that before.

As I ran down the Academy steps after my audition, my mum was waiting for me. Although she didn't really understand what the course was about or even why I wanted to do it, she could tell that it meant a lot to me, and the very fact that she had come to Glasgow with me showed I had her full support. My father was another matter. The only reason I had been allowed to apply at all was because the drama program offered a BA, in conjunction with Glasgow University, and those two letters seemed to dazzle my parents like rabbits in academic headlights, and somehow made the outrageous and dangerous idea of their son becoming an actor easier to bear.

I don't know what I would have done had I not been accepted

Alan Cumming performs at Cottiers Theatre, Glasgow in *Christmas is Cumming*, a fundraising event for the Royal Conservatoire 2019
(Photo: Robert McFadzean)

for drama school. I didn't have a backup plan for the rest of my life. I suppose I could have stayed on at DC Thomson where I had gone to work as a sub-editor after school. I liked it there. But I liked acting more. There was something about the doing of it that made me feel *alive* – well, since we're all obviously alive, I suppose *more* alive, heightened, energized. I guess pretending to be someone else is both a way to show others who you are and at the same time not fully have to present your true self. It's a constant duality of utter truth and utter deceit, and for me that was and is completely thrilling and addictive. And addictive is quite apposite actually, because I'm struck by how in trying to describe what it feels like for me to act, I want to reference the tingling, the rush, the giddy point of no return that we all get from our respective drug of choice, be it cigarettes or cocaine, tequila or chocolate, coffee or sex. Acting has been like that for me since the very beginning, and it still is.

    I was accepted. A letter was waiting for me from the Academy when I got home from work one evening a week or so later. And it wasn't just a letter of acceptance, it was an escape, a new life, a miracle.

Alan Cumming, BA Dramatic Studies, 1985
Author, actor and equality and human rights activist whose genre-spanning career has taken him everywhere from London's West End to Hollywood and Broadway.

SPOTLIGHT: Aaron Lee Lambert

(Photo: KK Dundas)

I came across the Royal Scottish Academy of Music and Drama by chance when I stumbled upon open auditions at a studio in New York City and happened to get into conversation with a lovely man who turned out to be Andrew Panton (Head of Musical Theatre in 2009).

I walked back to my day job brochure-in-hand, having no idea how much that encounter would profoundly change the course of my life.

I remember the audition quite vividly. I had come to Ripley Grier Studios that day to audition for a US regional theatre production of *Miss Saigon*, and while I had contemplated pursuing a Masters degree, I had never considered studying abroad. I sang a characterful William Finn song followed by 'Ol' Man River', learned a brief dance combination, and had a chat about where I was and wanted to go in my career. The ethos of the RSAMD felt in alignment with my needs and aspirations; it felt familiar yet challenging, and despite only being in the room for 20 minutes, I just knew it was the right fit.

When I finally arrived at the campus in Glasgow, my first impression of the building on Renfrew Street was that of a bustling hub of creativity. On any given day, I would walk down the corridor as I made my way to class and hear a xylophonist practicing, or an actor reciting Shakespeare, or opera singers perfecting a Mozart love duet. The atmosphere alone stimulated an amazing amount of development in my year group, both personal and artistic, and though we're now all spread around the world, it's always inspiring to see their diverse achievements and the varied work they're all doing in their respective countries, cities, and communities.

I have a lot of memories from my time studying but a highlight was taking a season of musicals to the Edinburgh Festival Fringe in 2009, one of which was *JERRY SPRINGER: The Opera*. It was such a fun production and a true ensemble piece, which was the perfect culmination of a year of intense growth alongside my peers. I played a nappy-wearing infantilist who later appeared as Jesus Christ in a fever dream, and I have the production photos to prove it!

While studying I was also fortunate enough to meet Andy and Wendy Barnes of Perfect Pitch Musicals, who would later go on to produce the hit musical *Six*. Some classmates and I were tasked with devising some material during a new musical workshop week, at the end of which we presented a few songs and a couple of scenes. Andy and Wendy attended that presentation, liked what they saw, and eventually supported me in developing that material into what would become a one-act musical called *From Up Here*, which made its World Premiere at South Hill Park in 2012. I continue to work with Perfect Pitch in a variety of capacities to this day, and I have the RSAMD to thank for initiating what has become a fruitful professional relationship.

The biggest lesson I learned during my time as a student – and one that I still carry with me – is the importance of the authenticity of one's voice. I don't mean one's singing or spoken voice in the literal sense, but more so who they are and what they have to say as an artist. Directors, producers, audition panels and audiences would much rather see an actor's unique light shining authentically at its brightest than someone trying to fit in to what they assume might be expected of them. As much as I can, I try to live by the motto: 'Work hard, never stop learning, and *do you*.'

I've had the pleasure of returning to the RSAMD – now the RCS – on a handful of occasions to work with students over the years, and it has always been a joyful experience. Most recently, it's felt full circle to step into the role of Director for the BA Musical Theatre production of Violet and the MA Musical Theatre production of Urinetown, both in 2021. My unique set of skills and experiences have proven to be well-suited to directing, and I've learned as much from my students as they have from me. It's fitting that, after all these years, the RCS continues to be a place where I learn, grow, and evolve.

Aaron Lee Lambert, MA Musical Theatre – Performance, 2009
Actor, writer and musical theatre star particularly known for his role in the West End production of *Hamilton*.

SPOTLIGHT: Richard Madden

(Photo: KK Dundas)

I feel incredibly lucky and privileged to have studied at the Royal Conservatoire. I wouldn't be here without it, and the opportunities it gave me. It was a safe place to start studying my craft and learning how to be an actor. It took a long time for me to be able to call myself an actor, and it gave me the confidence to do that, by making me feel like I always was one.

One of the reasons I applied to study here was because of how you

Richard Madden with students after receiving his Honorary Doctorate in 2019
(Photo: Robert McFadzean)

were described as a student on the acting course. It said I would be an actor-in-training, not simply a drama student, so before I even walked through the doors, I was an actor and I would be an actor while I was here. And hopefully I'd go on being an actor after I graduated.

The Conservatoire gave me the confidence to call myself an actor, it gave me a place to study my craft, it gave me the skills and encouragement to go out in the world and be the best that I could possibly be, to achieve what I wanted to and set out to do. This journey started here, and I'll be forever thankful and grateful and proud that I studied here.

Richard Madden, BA Acting, 2007
Golden Globe-winning actor and one of *Time* magazine's most influential people 2019. Screen credits include movies *Marvel's Eternals* and *Rocketman* and BBC's *Bodyguard*.

SPOTLIGHT: Ncuti Gatwa

(Photo: Robert McFadzean)

RCS's approach was very personal. It provides you with opportunities to develop in a way that you can't in the outside world. I felt very cared for. It was a safe space. Scotland has a thriving theatre scene and I think

Ncuti Gatwa performs alongside Tafline Steen
On the New Athenaeum stage in *Tartuffe*, 2012
(Photo: KK Dundas)

that being away from the mayhem of London allows you to concentrate on honing your craft.

Glasgow is one of the best places to live and study. The nightlife and people are wicked. The vibrancy of the city is infectious and you just have a good time. There is so much going on there and it's a beautiful city with real character – I would not have picked anywhere else.

Ncuti Gatwa, BA Acting, 2013
BAFTA Scotland Award-winning star of Netflix smash *Sex Education* who stars in the 2021 film *The Last Letter From Your Lover*.

Encomium, a Contemporary Performance Practice performance, 2016
(Photo: KK Dundas)

The New Athenaeum Theatre transformed into the Kit Kat Klub for Cabaret, 2015
(Photo: KK Dundas)

New students celebrate arriving at their new home during Freshers' Week in 2019 (Photo: Robert McFadzean)

9

One Conservatoire

WHILE INITIALLY THE schools of drama and music were discrete entities, in recent years the walls between the two have become much more porous and less defined. The first time both groups of students came together in performance was in 1997 at the institution's 150th anniversary gala, running from 8–11 October. Before a musical theatre degree was envisioned, the drama students mounted a performance of Stephen Sondheim's *Into the Woods*, while the music students provided accompaniment. The performance programme was accompanied by a reproduction of a letter from Sondheim himself, wishing the cast and crew would 'have fun with it' and thanking them for 'doing the show' (Sondheim correspondence, RCS Archives & Collections). It was an important watershed and introduced the concept of collaborative practice to the student journey.

In 2014, the Conservatoire instituted 'Bridge Week,' a period between formal classes where students of all disciplines are encouraged to collaborate and produce new work together. It continues to be an important catalyst for forging partnerships and creating a wider artistic community in which innovation and thoughtful artistry thrive. It was also to be the impetus behind the Conservatoire's wide-ranging curriculum reform.

SPOTLIGHT: Maggie Kinloch

(Photo: KK Dundas)

The Royal Conservatoire of Scotland is a place so dear to me, and so central to Scotland's cultural life. I studied there from 1972 to 1975; of course, it was RSAMD then. I worked there as a freelance teacher and director on and off during the '80s. In 2004 though, I became Director of Drama, eventually holding the post of Deputy Principal. In those ten years, I was tasked with leading a major Curriculum Reform project, and also with leading the Equality, Diversity and Inclusion work of the Conservatoire. You see, we had realised that the world of work for our graduates required excellent artists as it always had done, but now it also required them to be flexible, collaborative, socially aware, independent thinking, team-playing artists. We had to look at our curriculum and see where we could develop those skills in our students.

ONE CONSERVATOIRE

Curriculum reform was the most exciting and most difficult of tasks of course! I had spent decades travelling to over 30 countries to explore how artists were trained around the globe. As you would expect, there were many examples of amazing practice, and many that seemed to have missed the forward movement of time. I had the chance to see the very best, though, and here was the opportunity to bring some of that to our already great Conservatoire.

Of course, the disciplines of music, drama, filmmaking, ballet and production are utterly different. Musicians spend hours alone practicing their instrument before performing in any kind of ensemble; actors are in collaborative ensembles from day one. Dancers, filmmakers, and production artists all have varying ways and needs too.

Our Music and Drama schools were utterly different, with different timetables, assessment methods and schedules and even term dates! They each had their own school office, in fact. We were two schools in one building. Our first task, therefore, was to centralise all of the administration and to become one institution. That was achieved very effectively and led by my colleague Ewan Hainey.

That in place, we began the task of trying to build a curriculum that brought our five disciplines together. A curriculum that ensured all of the specialist teaching had its valued place, but also offered opportunities for students to collaborate with those in other disciplines.

We began with an Open Space day; a truly democratic event which posed the question, 'What will a new curriculum look like?'.

It took us four years before we were ready to roll it out, and a full four years to embed it. Eight years of designing, testing, commitment, imagination, heated debate, arguments even, excitement, joy and inspiration; eight years of staff, students, employers, external influences all thinking and working together.

Together we arrived at a shared curriculum which offered specialism and collaboration across all four years. Student-led Bridge Week was at the heart of it all and students just became so excited about it.

Underpinning all of that work, was a much looser but no less vital piece of work. I founded and led the Equality, Diversity and Inclusion

A reimagined performance of *A Midsummer Night's Dream*, produced as part of Bridge Week in 2016
(Photo: KK Dundas)

Forum. Any staff member or student who wanted to be there could come along to our meetings. There was a core of around 30 but overall maybe 50 were part of it. We had no budget at first, but managed to get a small budget of a few thousand pounds so that we could fund projects led by staff or students, which promoted Equality, Diversity and Inclusion.

As a Humanist, as a woman, as a gay woman, I know what it is to feel excluded, just because you are different in some way from the societal norm. I think that has driven a passion in me for fairness in our world, and to look at how we as human beings can proactively develop that further. Of course, an artist's job is to look at their world, and to comment on it via our work. To stimulate thought and creativity in our world.

So, we looked to find ways in which that could be woven into everyday life in our Conservatoire, and students' minds would be open to looking through that lens. We worked from the ground up, through our marketing images, the language we used, the composers and playwrights whose work we studied… the whole spectrum was discussed and challenged by that forum of committed and courageous people.

Introduction to Collaborative Practice was designed into Year One for every single student, and at its heart is the Universal Declaration of Human Rights. In interdisciplinary groups of around 12, students chose an article from the declaration and collaborated to create a performative response. It all culminated in a two day festival of the work. And what intelligent, moving, thought-provoking work would appear every year!

Change is never easy; it will always be resisted by some people, but there are also always opportunities for individuals to play their part if they want to. And our building was full of those brilliant folk!

During it all, Gerry Ramage of Glasgow-based theatre company Solar Bear approached me. His company make work for and by D/deaf artists. They had a terrific youth theatre as part of their company. There was nowhere in the UK at that time which provided conservatoire training for D/deaf actors. There is, however, plenty of talent in the D/deaf community. This was a barrier to access. It was simply unfair to all of the people of talent who could not find professional training just because they are D/deaf. Together RCS and Solar Bear designed the BA Performance in British Sign Language and English. It is the only degree of its kind in the UK. Two full cohorts of graduates are out in the industry now and are making real impact, winning awards and proving to us that we were right in bringing this training into being.

And because of the new curriculum and the strong element of choice with in it, every single student has the opportunity to learn BSL from the day they begin. That breaks down another barrier, and makes collaboration between D/deaf and hearing students possible.

I retired from RCS in 2015, curriculum reform complete and well bedded in. The eyes of conservatoires around the world were on us because we had done something they recognised they too would wish to do. The Conservatoire has consistently moved up the world rankings since the start of that work, now sitting comfortably in the top three. We aspired to top five, so that is really gratifying!

Maggie Kinloch
Professor Emerita and retired Deputy Principal.

A view from the sound desk as students rehearse for BA Musical Theatre showcase which was streamed online for the first time due to COVID-19 restrictions, 2021
(Photo: Robert McFadzean)

A Bridge Week performance in 2014
(Photo: KK Dundas)

10

Premières

OVER ITS LONG history, the Conservatoire has been responsible for an impressive number of firsts. Despite the inevitable jitters of opening night, the performing arts thrive on pushing boundaries and exploring the new. It isn't possible to list them all, and inevitably important innovations will be missed out here. These, however, represent some of the most recent, as remembered by those who were there.

In 1962, with advice from BBC Scotland, RCS became the first drama college in the United Kingdom that could boast a broadcast-specification television studio installed for the purposes of teaching acting to camera. Appropriately, the first broadcast made from the studio was a scene from James Bridie's play *The Anatomist*. Grainy black and white film footage of Hannah Gordon introducing then Principal, Henry Havergal, survives in the National Library of Scotland's Moving Image Archive – lasting proof of the only incidence he was known to be nervous in public.

In time, the studio was named the Groves Studio after John ('Johnny') Groves, former Deputy Director of the college, but in the 1960s it still felt completely new.

SPOTLIGHT: Tony Osoba

Tony Osoba pictured on set of Charles Endell Esquire in 1979
(Photo: AF archive – Alamy Stock Photo)

I was born in Glasgow (Stobhill Hospital) into a family of five. My parents met in Glasgow, my mother was Scottish and my father was Nigerian and, at the time, was working for a shipping company.

We lived in Glasgow and Renfrewshire where I attended school, Eastwood Secondary School in Renfrewshire. I was fascinated by literature, something my mother nurtured and, with the support of an excellent teacher, I developed a real interest in Shakespeare. Although I never took part in school plays or amateur dramatics, the idea of becoming an actor grew until, at 18, I went from imagining a career in the motor industry (cars are a great passion of mine to this day) to auditioning for drama school.

I attended the RSAMD from 1966–69. It was a three-year drama course that covered lessons in script work, fencing, classical theatre, musical theatre, radio and TV instruction and everything in between. It also taught us so much of the technique and discipline it takes to become an actor – the respect you need to have for everyone else involved in the project.

The Groves Studio was very new when I was studying and we had lessons there to train in the art of acting for camera – incredibly different from theatre where you learn to project your voice and exaggerate your movements. Here we had to learn how to perfect the level of performance for the camera, suddenly being conscious that a microphone was picking up your every movement.

This training meant that it didn't matter what job I was going to do – a film, a TV show, a radio drama – I always felt prepared thanks to my training.

Whenever I was working in the industry and looked back on my time at the college, it always struck me that I couldn't think of anywhere in the world that could offer a better and more thorough grounding in the profession. I feel very fortunate and privileged to have studied there. Colin Chandler led the drama school and he was a wonderful man; a gentle man who could command authority and who people respected greatly.

Colin Chandler, John Groves, Grace Matchett, John Colson, Toby Robertson and all the dedicated staff at the College combined to give invaluable, dedicated and nurturing instruction and encouragement to the students in their charge and care. There was very much the ethos that we were all equals; staff treated us as professionals and, in turn, everyone took their studies very seriously. It was an incredibly artistic place to be.

Undoubtedly, we all set off on our professional paths with a well-rounded knowledge and comprehensive training in all possible demands of our hoped-for careers.

Reflecting back, it is the people I remember rather than the performances… lifetime friendships were formed and everyone supported each other. The bond between the students was fostered by the staff. It

Students acting to camera in the newly completed Groves Television Studio, 1960s
(Photo: RCS Archives & Collections)

took me by surprise to learn later in life from other actors in the profession that not everywhere is like this, and we were lucky to have this at RSAMD.

Shortly after completing the three-year course at RSAMD, I headed down to London with a fellow graduate, the actor Peter Blake (née Ian Dempsey). Peter and I remained lifelong friends until his passing a few years ago. He was my Best Man when I married Sally in 1989 and I was his Best Man – twice.

Many of my male contemporaries at College went on to have very successful acting careers such as David Hayman, Alex Heggie, Dennis Lawson, Peter Blake and Jake d'Arcy (John Sinclair), with David Soames (David Woods, as was) gaining success as a producer and Gareth Waddell producing a successful young person's theatre production group. John Groves' daughter Alison was also in our class.

I was fortunate enough to have a very varied career including theatre,

The Groves Television Studio from the point of view of the control room, 1960s
(Photo: RCS Archives & Collections)

television, radio and the occasional film, and the good grounding delivered by the RSAMD was a very solid and comprehensive basis for any actor embarking on a career and has stood me in very good stead.

Although work was still on offer and overwhelming (but not always) challenging and enjoyable, I opted to retire as an actor in 2017 – over 50 years including Drama College seemed enough. You get less for murder, as the saying goes!

Tony Osoba, Diploma of Dramatic Arts, 1969

Tony's career as an actor took him from theatre and television to radio and film. He appeared in popular 1970s sitcom *Porridge*, soap opera *Coronation Street*, *The Bill* and *Hollyoaks*.

In 1993, the Royal Conservatoire of Scotland became the first conservatoire in the UK to be granted its own degree awarding powers by the Privy Council, with the Queen Mother receiving the very first degree *honoris causa*.

SPOTLIGHT: Isobel 'Bunty' Fowler

Isobel 'Bunty' Fowler at the conferment of the first honorary degree, given to Her Majesty, Queen Elizabeth, The Queen Mother, on 17 November 1994 at Clarence House
(Photo: Eric Thorburn)

I arrived at the RSAMD in 1981 initially as the accountant. In some ways, it was like entering the world of Dickens. I had come from a highly organised, commercial company where we had computerised accounts from stock orders right up to management accounts.

Initially I was attracted to the role by a very strange advert in the Glasgow Herald, which said RSAMD was looking for an accountant to 'computerise their manuscript ledgers'. A music college with manuscript ledgers! I thought that was funny and it grabbed my attention. I had been into computers since the '70s and had a lot of experience and I think that's why I got the job.

I walked in on the first day and no one seemed to know I was coming. I was put in this wee glass box with the outgoing accountant, and he opened the safe and took out all of these books, huge ledgers some of them going back to 1905. He put them in a row and put different pens across the top of them. They had shorthand written in the corner and it wasn't even proper Pitman shorthand so the typist couldn't read them.

I thought 'Do I stay, or should I go?' And then I thought 'Surely, I can't do anything but make it better?' and that was my attitude.

There were, of course, so many really good bits too, as I discovered. If you look back on that period and the quality of the alumni coming out of the institution, they were amazing. And yet, there was no Quality Assurance, no, nothing like that in place at all at that time. David Lumsden was the Principal when I arrived, and it was a very buzzy place but two distinct schools. There was the music, and there was the drama and Edward Argent was like the Principal of Drama, with Lumsden being the Principal of Music.

There was a lot to do and I wanted to be able to help them use their resources more effectively and in a way that more people could benefit from them. Before me, they were buying second-hand pianos on hire purchase, for example, so when I arrived I spent ages with each of the departments going through their budgets and helping them to get better use of the funds they had. It took a long time for people to realise that this wasn't about cutting their budgets but eventually when they saw that they might have funds left at the end of the financial year that allowed them to buy x or do y, they were delighted and you'd have thought they'd won the raffle.

When Philip Ledger arrived as Principal he challenged the concept of having the two very separate schools of music and drama, and very rightly said that he was the Principal of the 'RSAM and D' and he created a classic pyramid structure with a head of both music and drama. I think the build-up of opera really helped in pulling the two together more than anything else because the acting department could help, as could wardrobe and technical services. The funding models didn't help either, with first the Scottish Office and then the newly formed Scottish Funding Council funding music at a much higher rate than drama. But the way I looked at it and the way I did the budget was as a whole-academy budget, where all the money came in to one place and was used as it was needed. That meant that internally the drama school got a fair deal, but they never could see this because what was reported in the press was that the music courses were classed as getting much more funding.

As Director, my role covered anything that wasn't music or drama, so that meant it included HR, finance, buildings, IT, marketing, everything… and the trusts too. The trust was tiny at that time, an account with £6,000 in it that no one was quite sure what to do with. Those trusts are now worth more than £20 million.

Rita (Dr Rita McAllister, Director of the School of Music from 1986–96 and also Vice Principal to 2006) along with Russell Boyce, Deputy Director of the School of Drama, and I all worked extremely well together. We were a pretty persuasive force! When it came to degree-awarding powers, Rita was very much a driving force in that. In the late 1980s/early 1990s Quality Assurance began to raise its ugly head and we both went to a conference about it and decided we really did have to do something about it. At that point we had no structures for those things. Around the same time we were being courted by both Glasgow and Strathclyde Universities who both wanted us as their 'jewel in the crown'.

Before we had degrees at RSAMD, we had diplomas which used to be considered the top-notch qualification for musicians, but the world moved on and degrees became more desirable. Initially, David Lumsden set up BA degrees with Glasgow University, but in the late 1980s Margaret Thatcher said that the universities and HEIs which attracted students would be rewarded and many institutions started packing in students in massive numbers. We said we couldn't do that, we are a quality institution, not a volume market and if we did that the quality would go down. The Funding Council eventually agreed to keep us on what they had called 'a level playing field', which in effect meant that if there was a 2% increase in inflation, we should get a 2 per cent increase. At the same time, other universities were packing students in and, through the formula that was being used, they were getting 11 or 12 per cent increases while we got nothing. We called ourselves 'the zero percent club' and the Art School (Glasgow School of Art) was the same. I reckon that, over the course of a year or two, we lost the equivalent of more than £1 million, which is worth a lot more than £1 million these days.

On top of that, there were huge pressures for salary increases from the negotiating body for salaries for academic staff. The negotiations led to huge increases for higher education teaching staff, which RSAMD couldn't afford. We consulted our Staff Association and said there's a choice here; we can restructure and bring in more part-time staff as staff retire or pay higher salaries and lose jobs. The staff were extremely helpful and agreed we should come out of the negotiating body. We got to the stage where we either had to do this, or many staff would be made redundant or we would merge with Glasgow University. That's how near a knife edge it was. The staff saw the problem, we kept them in the loop and we got through it.

In terms of having our own degrees, at first we thought we'd go for Council for National Academic Awards (CNAA) degrees, but Philip Ledger was not in favour, so we plodded on with Quality Assurance and putting the building blocks in place we would need, and eventually it reached a point where it became obvious we could go for degree-awarding powers. Philip took that baton and he ran with it, and that was probably his crowning glory.

It was a long process started in 1991–92 and involved what was called the 'Drymen Group' of senior management (named after the Buchanan Arms in Drymen where we had weekends away) plus some academics. We thrashed out all the issues in what we soon realised was a huge process and I have to say so many universities and our sister institutions thought we were mental: how could a wee place like ours ever dream of having degree awarding powers? It took years, at least two years, but we went for it.

There was also a bigger group, the 'Degree-Awarding Powers Group', which included representatives from all across the institution. We met every Thursday from 12–1 and the Principal chaired the meetings. We all had tasks to do for the next week and everyone did them. We had massive staff meetings in the Athenaeum, with the Drymen Group sat on the stage giving presentations and answering questions from the staff. We took them with us all the way. We had focus groups, completely mixed across the departments, and it was really, really empowering. The whole staff were with us and we were all totally committed.

When the Scrutiny Panel for Degree Awarding Powers came in October 1993, they were quite critical of how light we were in professional services staff, but the reality was that we couldn't afford any more at the time. We had to convince them of how passionate all the staff were for this institution and I think that is still true.

We heard in 1994 that we were successful when a letter came to the Principal. We were all absolutely over the moon. Then the Registrar, Rita, and I had great fun designing the colour schemes for the graduation robes, and all of that. Philip Ledger had decided that the very first honorary doctorate should go to our Patron, who at the time was Queen Elizabeth The Queen Mother. Her Private Secretary said that the college secretary should accompany the Principal and that's why I ended up being invited. It was a wonderful experience, which took place in Clarence House. I loved it. We went down the night before and did a recce. We got in and were shown where we would be and what would happen. Next day. we had to be there in advance and her lady in waiting met us.

I took with me an old photograph of my husband's grandpa who had lived in Skye. When the Queen Mother was Duchess of York, she and the Duke had toured there on the Royal Yacht Britannia to see the dyeing process for the tweeds. We had a wonderful picture of him walking alongside the Queen Mother and all the school children lining up on both sides of the road cheering.

We had the ceremony. I had to put the hood over her head and I was terrified to touch her hair as it was long and curled up, and I kept practicing on Philip! Afterwards, they brought in the drinks and nibbles and the corgis were there, and I was called over to sit with the

Dame Janet Baker lodges a time capsule in the Renfrew Street
building site, September 1984
(RCS Archives & Collections)

Queen Mother and we looked at the picture. She said it brought back such happy memories for her and she remembered going there in the rowing boat and that they had all been singing 'Speed Bonnie Boat' whereupon she sang it to us. She was 95 at the time and had perfect pitch. That was a really special day.

In the midst of all of this we had a new building in Renfrew Street, a fantastic custom-built building, but full of problems left by the Contractor. The decision to find a new home for the Academy had been discussed right through the 1970s and into the 1980s. Everyone agreed we needed a new building, but there was a tussle between Edinburgh and Glasgow to give a site for it. Glasgow won out, the site was found, and the building was built between 1984–5 and 1987. Throughout the construction project, my involvement was paying out massive, massive

Dame Janet Baker with the Academy Symphony Orchestra conducted by Philip Ledger at the opening of the Renfrew Street building, 1988
(Photo: RCS Archives & Collections)

cheques, but I was involved more once we moved in because of all the problems. We compiled 1,500 user complaints. A lot concerned things like ventilation and lighting. Lots of niggling things. My room became an exhibition space for all the things that were failing. The Chairman finally brought in a surveyor to work through the complaints with me. Then we started getting leaks in the Guinness Room and we discovered the roof was failing. It took four years to replace it, but we were in court cases for ten years with the builders, so all of that was happening at the same time. We were booked into the High Court for 40 weeks. The case started and I gave evidence on the fifth day and then we settled.

In spite of all the problems, it was a fantastic building. I was the chair of the chief administrators group for all the UK conservatoires and as part of that I went round the other conservatoires and colleges. We were streets ahead of all of them in terms of our facilities and you couldn't help but be proud of what we had.

The Alexander Gibson Opera School photographed from
Cowcaddens Road in 1998
(Photo: KK Dundas)

We then started to think about creating a building for the Opera School. Up until then, Opera teaching was being delivered out of a building in Bath Street and at the same time the whole academy was expanding, bringing with it huge pressures on practice rooms.

So, we held a competition. I had read a book about Glynebourne and how they'd chosen their architect through a competition. We visited different architectural practices, collated the information and reported it to the Governors on the same day as the final three architects made their presentations. As Project Controller, I was pleased that the project ran on time and within budget. Initially we had had no money to pay for it, but through donations we started with £1 million. The National Lottery had only just started supporting arts organisations, so I went to see them. They were reluctant at first, assuming we got capital funding from the government, but after I revealed that we did not they were eventually persuaded. We were the first Higher Education institution to get a successful lottery bid. We got £2.5 million after presenting our case to a 12-strong assessment panel. The remaining £2 million was raised through private donations and fundraising events around Scotland. The Opera School was quite something, and we had such a fantastic opening week with rave reviews even from critics who had been very negative about us previously.

There were so many other new initiatives happening too, like Traditional Music, expanding the Junior Academy and sourcing student residences. Everything we did for RSAMD was a real team and community effort. I've believed in this all my life. If you don't take people with you, then you're fighting a losing battle. There were lots of challenges along the way but there was a lot of fun, I absolutely loved it. Every day I got up in the morning and I wanted to go to my work. I loved it.

Since I retired in 2005, being part of the RCS Trusts as a trustee has kept me connected and it's been lovely to see the journey continue and feel proud of, and in a way part of, current achievements.

Little did I know that responding to that advert to 'computerise the manuscript ledgers' would take me on the journey it did. But I loved every minute of it.

Isobel 'Bunty' Fowler
Retired Director of Finance and Administration.

The Alexander Gibson Opera School, the first purpose-built opera school in the UK, was completed and opened in 1998. Named after noted Conservatoire alumnus and founder of Scottish Opera Sir Alexander Gibson, the school was built on to the back of the then 11-year-old Renfrew Street building, expanding the footprint of the campus north to Cowcaddens Road.

SPOTLIGHT: Karen Cargill

(Photo: KK Dundas)

The opera school felt so modern, especially the atrium foyer. It really did feel glamorous, you know? Honestly, what a difference it made, having dedicated rooms just for the opera students. We felt like we were in a little bubble. We had our own studio theatre and practice rooms and we all loved RR13 – as it was known then – because the ceiling was so high, it had great acoustics and we all felt like we could sound like Jessye Norman.

We had a dedicated studio theatre where we would perform opera scenes and attend different classes which was such a wonderful space to have. One of the things I really enjoyed was singing in the coaching rooms on the ground floor, as people would walk past outside and sometimes would look in. Some of the other practice rooms were internal or were on higher floors so it gave you that contact with the outside world and I loved that.

My happiest times at RCS were in the opera school, without a shadow of a doubt. I did my best work and had an absolute ball with my teacher, Pat Hay, and loved being coached by Tim Dean.

I got to do three major productions. The first was playing the Old Prioress in *Dialogues of the Carmelites* by Francis Poulenc. As it was a student production, there wasn't really a budget for wigs and it wasn't really important for a dying nun to have a wig! So, we decided to put Vaseline and baby powder in my hair to make it look grey. In the scene where I died, I had to do a backflip off the bed and disappear while some of the stage managers, who were men dressed as nuns, flapped a sheet and did a scene change.

My parents were there on opening night and heard the person sitting next to them say 'oh my goodness, they've managed to capture her spirit leaving her body in a puff of smoke'.

It was all that talc in my hair – I should have been sponsored by Johnson & Johnson!

I also sang the role of Lucretia in *The Rape of Lucretia* by Benjamin Britten and Baba the Turk in *The Rake's Progress* by Stravinsky, directed by Steven Langridge, the Artistic Director of Glyndebourne who I'm working with at the moment.

I never thought I would ever have to shave my legs on stage or smash lots of crockery, the ultimate stress reliever! As Baba is a bearded lady, it was my first time wearing a beard. Some people said I looked like Brad Pitt in the film *Legends of the Fall*; in reality, I probably looked more like Kenny Rogers.

We did a photoshoot where I was Photoshopped into things like a perfume advert and into the famous picture of Nixon and Elvis at The White House, which I still have in my house. We had lots of performances, we travelled to Dubai to sing in concerts and went to the Royal Opera

Karen Cargill performs work by Verdi and Wagner
with RCS students at the City Halls, 2012
(Photo: KK Dundas)

for the first time, where we sang at the Linbury Theatre, which had just opened. What amazing experiences, it was such a happy time.

I was of the generation who watched *Fame*, so going from Arbroath to RCS as a 17-year-old was amazing. I was waiting for people to start dancing on taxis outside!

But it was terrifying. I remember standing in the corridor outside the Fyfe Lecture Theatre and thinking 'oh no, no, no, no, no. This is not for me. I'm not good enough for this'. I called my parents and said 'I need to come home. This is a mistake'.

I'd just been given my timetable and hadn't even had a class. Once I started singing and getting into the actual performing that made a huge difference because that's what we were all there to do. To be nurtured, to be creative, and there were lots of members of staff who were so supportive and caring and made me feel calm.

I left when I was 25 and still have friendships I made at opera school.

Those were seminal years, going through shared experiences that could feel so exposing and nerve-wracking.

I remember being in the corridor outside the Stevenson Hall before a performance, and it felt like the worst place in the world! But once my feet were on that wooden floor and I could look up to the wee lighting booth, I'd be in my happiest place.

Now, as Interim Head of Vocal Performance, it feels like I've come full circle. I can use that experience to help the students explore their own practice.

That fear I experienced is something that we all feel at some stage and it's okay – it's natural. We're lucky to be in the position to feel it, to embrace it and use it as energy. As much as I was terrified, I was encouraged to tell my story and that's what we're all here to do. When you're in a place where you get to do that, it's phenomenal.

Karen Cargill, M Mus (Opera), 2001
Internationally acclaimed mezzo-soprano who has graced the world's finest stages from the Royal Opera House to the Metropolitan Opera in New York.

In 1999, the then Academy created a new BA course in Contemporary Theatre Practice (now Contemporary Performance Practice). A ground-breaking addition to the syllabus, the course is an interdisciplinary performance-making degree which trains students to create new and original performances which sit outside the normal strictures of traditional theatre.

Merging the worlds of acting, directing, writing, performance art and social responsibility, CTP/CPP students are encouraged to challenge norms, break down barriers and to affect change in the world around them through creative, collaborative and socially engaged performance. It is thought to have been the first course of its kind in the country, although there are now many others that share the name.

SPOTLIGHT: Johnny McKnight

(Photo: Drew Farrell)

The Academy was almost like a mythical place, that place where 'actors' went. I really didn't know much about it. In all honesty, I had no idea what to expect when I applied. I had studied a year on a law degree before drama school, so I genuinely thought it might be like that. I was shocked at the hours, how much more demanding it was than I could have ever expected,

   I auditioned three times, three consecutive years. I think it's important for people coming in to try and remember that. Keep going. To be in our business we need talent, yes, but to stay in it you need resilience and perseverance. Don't give up. And each time you have to bounce back, bounce back harder. Believe in yourself.

Each time I didn't get in was gutting, but I kept going back because, for me, it was the only place I wanted to study. I wanted to stay in Scotland. However, I am a big believer in 'what's for you won't go by you' and the year I got in was the year I was supposed to be part of. It was the first year of the then Contemporary Theatre Practice course and, looking back, even the audition was the right thing for me – you had to devise your own piece.

My piece was about how I'd auditioned here three times and it was time for the audition panel to stop asking me to run around a room like a prehistoric animal and let me in. I think I also showed them how good I was at playing a tree. Thankfully they got my humour and I was accepted onto the course. It felt like a fit, and thankfully it was.

Being a student at that time, I just remember it being so exciting and new, a total eye-opener. I was so ill-informed when it came to theatre before I started studying. I think my knowledge amounted to a few musicals. Everything was challenging and demanding and brilliantly informative. My year group were the most eclectic, passionate and brilliant people, and became friends who I still work and socialise with. I think when you go on a journey like that together it bonds you for life.

I have so many highlights from my time at drama school. I went from working in a supermarket to touring pieces of work to schools; devising shows based on Classical Greek Drama; performing as a street theatre band in Buchanan Street (and somehow it didn't rain!); going to Amsterdam to support our year group who'd been selected to take their own show out there; doing my first directing piece with Dame Judi Dench (okay, it was a mannequin called Dame Judi, but hey ho); working with a community group of line dancers and us all terribly trying to keep up with them on the dance floor. There are so many memories, and so many learning opportunities that came from them, that even now I take inspiration from in my work.

My favourite lesson, or rather quote that was always used (I just googled, it comes from anthropologist Angeles Arrien) is this: 'Show up. Pay attention. Tell The Truth. Don't attach to the results'. I think that's a brilliant lesson, not just in our work, but for life.

My career has taken many different directions and it absolutely all came from my training at the Academy. Our training wasn't just about being on stage and performing; it was about how to be autonomous. We had to learn every area of making work – we took on stage management; marketing; directing; devising as a team; taking the step to writing our own work; facilitating workshops; devising classes or process drama. It all added up, and it gave me confidence to know that saying YES is important. To know that you have to venture into the unknown with a thirst to learn and also a curiosity to see what you can bring to each project. Before I started studying, I could only ever imagine performing, because it was the only job I could visibly see; studying at the Academy opened my eyes to the full range of what I could engage in. I still try to carry that with me, that sense of possibility, of knowing that being uncomfortable and challenged means you are learning and developing and that maybe, just maybe, something brilliant is just around the corner.

Johnny McKnight, Contemporary Theatre Practice, 2002
Writer, director, educator and performer whose work spans theatre and television. Described as the 'vanguard of post-modernist panto' with 23 productions under his belt.

The BA in Modern Ballet was launched in 2009 under the artistic direction of Paul Tyers and in close association with the national ballet company, Scottish Ballet. In so doing, RCS became the first conservatoire in the UK to offer training in all the major disciplines of the performing arts.

SPOTLIGHT: Jamie Reid

Jamie Reid performs in the BA Modern Ballet Graduation Showcase, 2015
(Photo: KK Dundas)

I started in 2012, so the course was only three years old then. The best thing for me was being from Glasgow, as I didn't have to move away from home to continue my training, which would've been the case before the course was set up. Pre-2009 for a young Scottish dancer, it was guaranteed that you'd have to move to London or elsewhere if you wanted to go forward and have a professional career. Having the ballet programme in my home city, whilst still being able to get the same high standard of training as elsewhere, was the best of both worlds for me.

  Being able to train full time and pushing myself every day was what I really enjoyed the most. Especially when our assessments were done,

Paul Liburd OBE teaches a ballet masterclass in the dance studios, 2018
(Photo: Robert McFadzean)

and we would start rehearsals for about six weeks leading up to the graduation performance at the end of every year.

In my first year, we performed a piece at Tramway called *MONAD*. It was a collaboration between RCS and The Glasgow School of Art to celebrate the 100th anniversary of *The Rite of Spring*. That was my first ever ballet performance, so that is still a special memory. The graduation performances at the end of each year were also always great, especially my final one.

We had a few guest artists over my three years, but one in particular I remember was Paul Liburd, who was a former dancer with Scottish Ballet and Rambert. That guy was an absolute machine! He came for a week when I was in second year to take classes and teach repertoire he had done in his career . That week for me was brilliant, just to see how hard working you really had to be each day.

The Wallace Studios were definitely world-class, from the quality of the floors to the big studio sizes. That is one of the appealing things about studying at RCS – how high the standard of facilities is. I bumped into the cast of *Still Game* one morning during the summer when I had to go in and pick some stuff up – they were using the studios to rehearse for their shows at the Hydro, so I was absolutely buzzing that day!

Training your technique, learning different repertoire and also the performance opportunities helped massively when I turned professional. Having the chance in third year to go over to the Scottish Ballet and do company class every other Saturday was also a massive bonus, as it gave you that wee insight into a professional environment. I do now miss no longer having Saturdays off though!

Jamie Reid, BA Modern Ballet, 2015
Jamie Reid is a BA Modern Ballet graduate and Artist with Scottish Ballet.

The BA Performance in British Sign Language and English was the first of its kind, not only in the UK but in Europe. A course developed in partnership with Solar Bear Theatre Company, the degree is designed for individuals who identify as D/deaf or hard of hearing and teaches students to be both actors and makers of new work. The degree was first launched in 2015.

Ciaran Stewart was one of the first students to enrol in the programme, and made history in 2018 when he, alongside nine of his fellow classmates, walked across the Stevenson Hall and collected his degree certificate. Since graduating, Ciaran has worked extensively in both TV and theatre, performing with companies including Headlong, Paines Plough, Sheffield Crucible and, most recently, he appeared in the BBC drama *Traces*. Ciaran Stewart was one of the first students to enrol in the programme,

Claire Wetherall, BA Performance in British Sign Language and English performs in The Assumption, a co-production between RCS and Solar Bear performed at Tramway in November 2020
(Photo: Robert McFadzean)

and made history in 2018 when he, alongside nine of his fellow classmates, walked across the Stevenson Hall and collected his degree certificate. Since graduating, Ciaran has worked extensively in both TV and theatre, performing with companies including Headlong, Paines Plough, Sheffield Crucible and, most recently, he appeared in the BBC drama *Traces*.

SPOTLIGHT: Ciaran Stewart

(Photo: Julie Howden)

The reason I chose to study BA Performance in BSL and English at RCS was because of the course content – it taught you to be an actor, a theatre-maker, how to make film… it was exciting and there was nothing else like it out there. To be part of the first cohort of graduates is truly special and it was an honour to be part of something that is so important within the arts. I always look back at my time at RCS with such fondness.

My highlights of studying at RCS were performing in Scavengers (written by Davey Anderson) and the graduation showcase; I loved that as I got to work with two pieces of text. I really enjoyed being around my classmates – it felt like a really exciting time.

RCS really taught me how to balance my work. It pushed me further

Scavengers by Davey Anderson performed by the Conservatoire's first BA Performance in BSL and English cohort, 2017
(Photo: Julle Howden)

as an actor and, even in my final year, I was still learning loads about myself and that's something that I still carry now. It also taught me discipline and I find that whenever I am working, I'm confident in my abilities. RCS gave me challenges that I never thought I could do… at the moment I'm working on a promenade performance, and if it wasn't for RCS pushing me, I don't think I would have ever done that!

Every time I go for an audition, I always get asked about the course – I think that is a true reflection of how important and valuable the training is considered in the industry. The BA Performance course continues to evolve and it offers amazing opportunities for students.

Right now, it is a challenging time for the arts, but artists are adaptable. Value your mental health and look after yourself. Sometimes you need to take a breather to ask yourself what it is you want to be. Be confident and know your worth – you have a voice so don't be afraid to use it.

Ciaran Stewart, BA Performance in BSL and English, 2018
Ciaran Stewart is an actor and a graduate of the pioneering BA Performance in British Sign Language and English degree at RCS.

BA Filmmaking shoot on Loch Lomond
(Photo: Robert McFadzean)

The Scottish National Academy of Music

St. George's Place, Glasgow

The Scottish National Academy of Music publicity brochure at the change of name, c. 1927
(Photo: RCS Archives & Collections)

11

What's in a Name?

OVER THE YEARS, RCS has flown various banners and brandings.

In 1927, the Glasgow Athenaeum School of Music changed its name to the Scottish National Academy of Music (SNAM). Student numbers had remained broadly constant, hovering around 1,600 when rebranded as SNAM, just as they had when the Glasgow Athenaeum opened its doors in 1847. The Athenaeum College of Commerce, which had been running concurrently with the music school, was now completely separated and would eventually come to form part of the University of Strathclyde. William Gillies Whittaker (known as the Viking, only sometimes affectionately) was appointed Principal of SNAM in 1933, and was simultaneously appointed Gardiner Chair of Music at the University of Glasgow; the roles would remain linked for decades until the demands of both became too overwhelming to be occupied by one person.

Whittaker was a Bach scholar at a time when the Baroque composer was considerably less well-known than he is today. He founded the Bach Cantata Choir at the SNAM with the sole purpose of performing as many of Bach's 200+ surviving cantatas as they could programme.

In 1941, Ernest Bullock (known as Deadly Ernest by the students) took over the dual role of Principal of the SNAM and Gardiner Chair of Music. Bullock was an organist and composer who had been entrusted with the arrangements of fanfares and incidental music at the coronation of King George VI in 1937 as part of his duties as organist and Master of the Choristers at Westminster Abbey. He would reprise this duty in 1953 at the Coronation of

Her Majesty The Queen Mother painting scenery
in the Technical and Production Arts Department, 1964
(Photo: RCS Archives & Collections)

Queen Elizabeth II. The original handwritten manuscripts from both occasions are now held by the Royal Conservatoire of Scotland's Archives & Collections.

It was under Bullock's leadership that the Scottish National Academy of Music became the Royal Scottish Academy of Music in 1944, with Queen Elizabeth the queen consort (later the Queen Mother) as patron. Given the Principal's personal royal connections, it was perhaps an inevitable turn of events.

SPOTLIGHT: Maura Coll

(Photo: Maura Coll)

In 1961, I had my first glimpse of the Royal Scottish Academy of Music. On arriving for my audition, I entered the Academy from St George's Place (now known as Nelson Mandela Place) and up the staircase into a rather impressive foyer. That is where I first met Pat McMahon, who was also having her audition. She introduced herself to me and with her outgoing and friendly personality, she helped calm my nervousness by giving me a liquorice sweet to clear my throat! (I am delighted to see that she has recently been awarded a well-deserved honorary fellowship of the Royal Conservatoire.) After a successful audition – and gaining a place to study voice as my first subject at the prestigious Academy – the blazer and scarf were duly purchased from Rowans in Buchanan Street. Rowans was an outfitters which supplied clerical garb, boarding school uniforms and university blazers. I thought the Academy blazer was the best of all, with its beautiful gold thread and maroon badge featuring St Cecelia, the patron saint of musicians. I have to say I wore it with great

Royal Scottish Academy of Music school blazer and scarf, donated to RCS Archives & Collections by Maura Coll in 2017
(Photo: Robert McFadzean)

pride – even on holiday!

I was privileged to have had Winnie Busfield as my singing teacher, someone to whom I owe so much and whom I remember with great fondness. I have memories also of regularly fetching her a snack (a date sandwich!) for lunch from 'The Buffet' in the basement, which is now part of the restaurant, Amarone. Part of the basement was also used as a venue for opera classes which were directed by Dr Barritt and, for these classes, we were joined by the drama students.

One of the highlights of the year was the opera production. I remember taking part in a number of notable performances – for example, *The Carmelites* and *Carmen*. Charles Escourt was my excellent piano teacher and gentle Marie Dare taught me cello, enabling me to be introduced to orchestral participation. However, it was not easy transporting my cello to and from Dumbarton on a bus or train!

I can recall vividly the Queen Mother's visit in 1964 where she approved the amalgamation of the RSAM and the College of Dramatic Art, which then became the RSAMD (Royal Scottish Academy of Music and Drama). In the Stevenson Hall, she was entertained with a concert which included a performance by Jack Keany and Jean Hutchison on piano.

These are a few reminiscences of very happy and fruitful days, with a rather special group of students and teachers, some with whom I am still in touch.

Maura Coll, DRSAM, 1965
Retired teacher and choral director (specialising in sacred music)

Having taught drama formally as part of the curriculum for 18 years, the Royal Scottish Academy of Music finally incorporated the school into its title, becoming the Royal Scottish Academy of Music and Drama (RSAMD) in 1968. Curiously, by this time student numbers had significantly decreased, with a shift away from part-time tuition into a more professional and full-time class arrangement. In 1967, the year before the change of name, there were only 276 student subscriptions (227 for music and 49 for drama). The change of name was to precipitate an even more profound change, with another move of building.

Continued expansions in student provisions and teacher numbers (partly necessitated by the increased range of courses on offer and partly by the professionalisation of teaching with awards of diplomas) meant that the Academy had outgrown its buildings on Buchanan Street and Nelson Mandela Place. Custom built facilities were completed in 1987, 99 years after the completion of the old Athenaeum, and the Academy moved wholesale later that year. The move was marked by an 'End of an Era Gala' in the Buchanan Street building, organised by Katie Berker and Eona Craig, and among the performers were John Cairney, Maureen Beattie, David Hayman, Alan Cumming, Una McLean and Andy Stewart. The gala raised nearly £3,000, which was divided between various local and national charities.

The new building on Renfrew Street was designed by renowned architect Sir Leslie Martin whose accomplishments include the Royal Festival Hall in the Southbank Centre, London, and was formally opened in March 1988 by the late Queen Mother in her capacity as royal patron. The celebrations were led by internationally renowned mezzo-soprano Dame Janet Baker, who was President of the Academy at the time.

By the 1990s, student numbers were again on the increase, averaging nearer 400. The Renfrew Street campus was designed with expansion in mind and was meant to be fit for purpose on a 100 year forward plan. As already seen, it didn't take long to out-grow it.

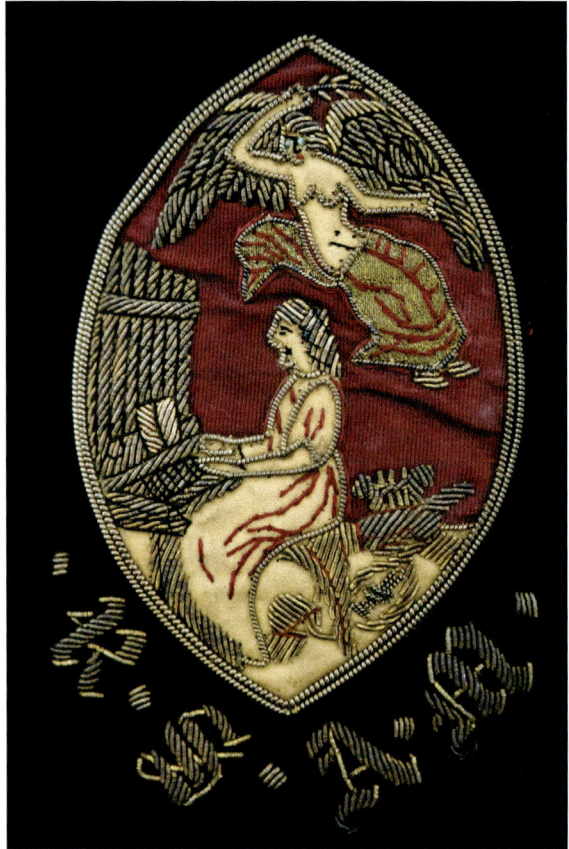

Close up feature of St Cecilia, patron saint of music, on the Royal Scottish Academy of Music blazer
(Photo: Robert McFadzean)

Today, average student numbers sit around the levels seen in the early to mid-19th century levels: around 1,200.

In 2009, the addition of degrees in Jazz and Modern Ballet prompted yet another change of name. It being thought that the Royal Scottish Academy of Music and Drama and Dance was a bit of a mouthful, under Principal John Wallace 'RSAMD' became the 'Royal Conservatoire of Scotland' in 2011.

Acting student Ainsley Jordan performs as the Snow Queen in 2016
(Photo: KK Dundas)

Sam Heughan and His Royal Highness The Duke of Rothesay on the New Athenaeum Theatre stage during a visit in 2019 (Photo: Robert McFadzean)

Work of a costume designer as they work on costume for the upcoming performance of *Festen*
(Photo: KK Dundas)

SPOTLIGHT: John Wallace

(Photo: KK Dundas)

From the time I first came to the RSAMD in the old buildings to work for Bob Inglis who organised the concert series and allied performance classes in the 1980s, I had fallen in love with the collegiate atmosphere of the old Academy. There seemed to me to be a very flat hierarchy and the whole place worked like clockwork, a masterpiece of Scottish organisation. It was Bob who alerted me to the history of the RSAMD, and its incredible historic holdings, which at that time were beginning to dissipate into private hands, as is the way of all things. Happily, the setting up of the archives reversed that trend. I had been part of Scotland's exodus of people. I left Scotland from school to go to university in England and never returned except to visit relations and do cameo musical roles with Scottish orchestras and ensembles playing my trumpet.

When the Academy moved up to Renfrew Street in 1988, Bob persuaded the then Principal, Sir Philip Ledger, to book me as one of the regular International Visiting Artists, and I built up a great relationship with the students and teachers. It is difficult to express the excitement of those early days in the new building, with Glasgow Year of Culture 1990 acting as a catalyst to project Glasgow's unique character and culture to the world. With the opening of the Glasgow Royal Concert Hall in that year, Renfrew Street became a veritable Avenue of the Arts, something that the City Fathers, always a bit slow on the uptake, have still to recognise. During the 1990s I became preoccupied with running a portfolio career in London, which included running the brass department at the Royal Academy of Music, and the RSAMD and I went our separate ways.

In 2002, when I became the first Scottish Principal for a hundred years, I was astonished to be chosen, and my previous experience had filled me full of idealism for the institution. I was also amazed by how well the place was run and how good it was. It was easily the finest institution with the best governance I had ever worked for. It had its own degree awarding powers which it had gained a decade earlier and was far ahead of any other institution I had taught at, except perhaps the Sibelius Academy in Helsinki. However, reputation is often built on location, and institutions in big cities like London and New York, which accrue cultural capital without ever having to try, have a natural assumption of superiority, which does not always survive closer scrutiny. So, with Philip Ledger's words ringing in my ears that my job as Principal would be to be its 'heid bummer', I set about repositioning the RSAMD's self-esteem, as well as the perception of this esteem in the crowded field of its international competitors. This work had been primed by David Lumsden and Philip Ledger from the 1980s and powered by Bunty Fowler, Rita McAllister and others doing much of the legwork.

The major stumbling block to the RSAMD's own psyche and its personal self-regard was that it was a divided institution, with Drama funded at less than 50 per cent of the rate of 'conservatoire' music, and cross-subsidised from the RSAMD Trust to equalise the amount of money spent on each student. Added to this, Drama had just got an unsatisfactory appraisal from the Quality Assurance Agency right before I arrived, and morale was pretty low. There's nothing like money, or the lack of it, to spread discontent and so there was much work to be done.

I never liked the word 'conservatoire' initially, thinking it was 'poo-bah'. But it was during the six years of day and night struggle – one that took years off my life and turned me into a gibbering wreck at times – that I became convinced that the 'conservatoire' word was part of the winning argument. After a six-year 'swimming up Niagara Falls every day' campaign with our funders, our RSAMD teams finally amassed the arguments and implementation plans for a sequence of strategies centred on creating the future for performance, which led to conservatoire funding for Dance, Drama, Music, Screen and Technical Arts. This brought the whole institution into a situation of parity of esteem, both internally and externally.

The conservatoire name change helped our self-perception and the perception of others. This umbrella word helped us to get closer to equality. Equity even; very difficult to achieve in the 21st century and becoming more difficult by the minute. But I was always convinced that the investment in teaching at the highest level implied by 'conservatoire funding' in and across every discipline for a sustained period of time would bear fruit, and this has proved to be the case. Although I feel, and always will feel, nostalgia for the old RSAMD, the RCS is a fitting incarnation of our beloved institution for the present times in which we live.

John Wallace
Professor Emeritus and retired Principal.

John Wallace puts the finishing touches to new building signage as RSAMD changes its name to the Royal Conservatoire of Scotland, 2011
(Photo: KK Dundas)

12

Change is a Constant

IN THE WORLD of the performing arts, nothing is static. What may seem to the outside world like a torturous last-minute panic is more often than not a partially controlled chaos; it's an environment in which creativity and innovation thrive.

It is much the same for the institution itself; change and a constant forward momentum drives RCS to continually challenge itself, push at unopened doors and step into the new. That is not to suggest that it's often done calmly.

As the Royal Conservatoire of Scotland looks forward to the next 175 years, it does so with a resilience of spirit and a mind open to the shifting landscape of the performing arts. Change is not only a constant, but also the story of the institution's own long history; it is what keeps the arts alive and fresh, challenging and new.

BA Modern Ballet student rehearses a contemporary dance piece
(Photo: KK Dundas)

Coda

Coda (noun): A separate passage at the end of something such as a book or a speech that finishes it off; in music, the final part of a fairly long piece which is added in order to finish it off in a pleasing way.

We find our greatest bliss in moments of collective effervescence. It's a concept coined in the early 20th century by the pioneering sociologist Émile Durkheim to describe the sense of energy and harmony people feel when they come together in a group around a shared purpose. Collective effervescence is the synchrony you feel when you slide into rhythm with strangers on a dance floor, colleagues in a brainstorming session, cousins at a religious service or teammates on a soccer field. And during this pandemic, it's been largely absent from our lives. Dr Adam Grant, *New York Times*, 10 July 2021

The Renfrew Street campus bathed in red as part of the #LightItInRed awareness campaign of the fragility of the arts during the COVID-19 lockdown
(Photo: Robert McFadzean)

ROYAL CONSERVATOIRE OF SCOTLAND: RAISING THE CURTAIN

Friday 13 March 2020

In spite of the looming cloud over Thornhill in the Scottish Borders, it was far from being an inauspicious day. There was a performance to prepare for; the singers and musicians had rehearsed for a final time, before eating a light supper and donning their concert dress. The audience was assembling, also smartly dressed, equally excited at the experience of being in Drumlanrig Castle, one of the finest examples of 17th century Renaissance architecture in Scotland, a fairy-tale pink sandstone edifice with breathtaking views across the Nith Valley. With the benefit of hindsight, the scene embodied a fin-de-siècle moment. A last hoorah before the storm. That evening, a small party from the Conservatoire (including the Principal, Professor Jeffrey Sharkey, the Chair, Nick Kuenssberg, and some guests) were at a dinner and recital in the castle. They were savouring the inspiring conclusion of a retreat that a small group of Vocal Studies students had just undertaken under the tutelage of mezzo-soprano Karen Cargill, RCS alumna and Associate Artist. The residency itself had offered a deep dive into Robert Schumann's *Liederkreis* song cycle, culminating in that memorable performance for guests, hosted by the Duke of Buccleuch. Over three music-filled days of preparation, the group had immersed themselves in this music, exploring it in a way that Karen Cargill reflects was 'extraordinary'. 'It was the most special time, I loved it,' she would reflect afterwards.

At its heart, the residency had focused on Schumann's *Liederkreis*, Op. 39, a classic composition, regarded as core repertoire for almost every singer. Through the cycle's twelve vignettes, Schumann (and in turn these students) explored the recurrent and intertwining themes of loss and loneliness, mystery, menace and wistful reverie. This project was a beginning, the first in a new collaborative partnership between the Conservatoire and the Buccleuch Living Heritage Trust. But it was in many ways also a poignant end; one of the last live performances with singers and musicians together in a room with their audience, in a time that would eventually become framed as 'Life before Covid'…

A shot of the digital work created by dance students at home during the COVID-19 pandemic

In the days that followed, it became increasingly clear that the Coronavirus outbreak was going to have enormous impact on the staff and students of the Conservatoire. Since the beginning of March 2020, the Principal and the Conservatoire Senior Management Team (CSMT) had been holding regular Covid Update meetings. Along with staff in every area of operations, they started formulating and reformulating contingency plans as information became available. But it was only on the weekend of 13–15 March that, with a sense of incredulity, it finally dawned on us how severely we would be impacted by this new virus. Like almost every other part of society, the Conservatoire would be affected in many ways – some of which we just didn't understand back then.

That Sunday afternoon (15 March 2020), students and staff were advised by an urgent email from the Principal that, 'given the continued spread of the COVID-19 outbreak and in line with our colleagues across the Scottish Higher Education Sector', RCS would suspend all face-to-face teaching, move to distance learning, and suspend all performances, concerts and public events until further notice. The following Friday, exactly a week after the uplifting joys of the Drumlanrig Castle experience, the Principal announced the Conservatoire would close its doors at 4pm for what would turn out to be the longest period in its history. An institution that had remained open through two World Wars would, on this occasion, like so many other institutions and organisations, be locked up.

Overnight, an institution defined by the seemingly ceaseless energy and activity of its inhabitants fell dark and silent. In a message to the community that day, Jeff Sharkey informed staff and students that all learning and teaching activity for Term 3 would be delivered online, with the RCS campus remaining closed 'until further notice'. He said that the CSMT would continue to meet regularly (virtually) and would issue twice-weekly bulletins to students and staff on Monday and Friday afternoons. He ended his message by saying:

> This is a very anxious and unsettling time for us all. None of us has been here before and I appreciate that we all need time to adapt to what, for the next while, will be our new normal. Please take the time to take a breath and focus on your family, friends and loved ones. These are exceptional circumstances and we do need to take care of ourselves and of each other.

Understanding the strong need to keep an RCS community of artists – one which thrives in normal times on multitudinous interpersonal creative moments – connected through a time of enforced isolation led the External Relations team to look for virtual solutions. As the clock ticked towards Conservatoire closure, plans came together.

On Monday 23 March, the day that Prime Minister Boris Johnson announced the first national lockdown, the Conservatoire launched 'RCS at Home', a digital platform with a mission to ensure an RCS community was able to continue to share its love of the performing and production arts with each other and as wide an audience as possible.

In the months that followed, thousands tuned in to RCS at Home

A team of volunteers from the Students' Union
drop off essential supplies to self-isolating students
during Freshers' Week, 2020
(Photo: Robert McFadzean)

to watch everything from world premieres of devised work to classical theatre filmed and streamed from the New Athenaeum stage. There were knowledge exchange discussions, a sharing of research and international masterclasses. A concert series developed by the Artistic Planning team, 'RCS Presents' provided an international platform for the School of Music's students, staff and alumni.

> Sitting at home isn't where you'd expect to enjoy world-class performing arts, but the Royal Conservatoire of Scotland is aiming to shift people stuck at home away from Netflix and towards something more highbrow with their digital platform, RCS at Home.
>
> Rachel Hall, *The Guardian*, 9 April 2020

In the early days, performances were essentially domestic in form, self-recorded by the artists themselves in the living rooms and kitchens where they were dealing with lockdown. As lockdown life continued and as the technical skills and a sense of adventure developed, so too did the art flow on to wider, bolder landscapes, as RCS at Home became an artistic window to the world for a physically closed Conservatoire, attracting many thousands of viewers from 95 countries.

The students and staff of RCS also responded to the early shockwaves and ongoing practical challenges of digital learning through trial and error, hard work and a great deal of resilience. Term 3 of the 2019/20 Academic Year was delivered entirely online. As the months went on and lockdown proper distilled down to 'Levels' of restrictions, thoughts turned across the Conservatoire to the possibilities, as well as the enormous challenges, of resuming elements of in-person learning and teaching deemed critical to student assessment.

25 May 2020

In the midst of the global pandemic, the horrific murder of African American George Floyd at the hands of a police officer on the streets of Minneapolis put the absolute injustice of systemic and institutional racism firmly on the agenda across the world, RCS included. Published in August 2020, the RCS's first Anti-Racism Action Plan, led by Deputy Principal Dr Lois Fitch and produced alongside staff and students. It is a 'living document', one which aims to make meaningful change for students now and for generations of students in the future.

> The more versatility and diversity there is in the curriculum, the more well-rounded an artist you're going to be. At that point, whatever background you're from, whatever you've been exposed to, your artistic personality has something in it of everything you've ever encountered. The shift is happening and that is encouraging.
>
> Dr Lois Fitch, Deputy Principal

The Bacchae was the first performance held during the COVID-19 pandemic and the cast and creative team had to work within strict guidelines to ensure social distancing was in place throughout the entire rehearsal and production process
(Photo: Robert McFadzean)

Over the summer of 2020, against a seemingly optimistic external backdrop of Eat Out to Help Out, a mammoth internal task began: to prepare and co-ordinate a campus, its programmes, professional services and operations to run efficiently and, most importantly of all, safely within restrictive government and public health guidelines. It was frustratingly complex work, in both a strategic and operational sense, even to enable limited in-person teaching and learning to take place. A substantial number of changes to the campus were required to ensure it was a safe learning environment where strict social distancing could be maintained at all times. The changes ranged from a draconian reduction of numbers on campus (fewer than 5 per cent at any given time), to creating one-way systems around campus, introducing mask-wearing, installing handwashing stations, transforming spaces into new performance venues and student break-out areas and ensuring every room had strict capacities.

RCS was encouraged to become a Covid-considerate community, with students and staff urged to be kind to each other and to keep each other safe. Throughout the entire Academic Year 2020/21 there was not a single reported case of Covid transfer on campus, a demonstration of a successful combination of hard work and good will.

Wellbeing was a huge priority and a Welcome Home team was formed to support students returning to RCS in the strangest of times. The team comprised of staff from External Relations, Academic Administration Services, the Students' Union President, John Craig and alumna Joanne Bell, and was supported by the Students' Union officers, Front of House staff and staff volunteers from across the Conservatoire. The project morphed into a Home from Home programme offering ongoing support to students across both term time and the holidays in a variety of forms. Members of the Front of House team were redeployed to deliver groceries and offer one-to-one telephone support lines; academic and professional services staff from across the institution also presented online cook-a-longs, organised student and staff quizzes and led safely-distanced guided walks – all manner of activity designed to create multiple points of connection, if not contact, right through to a Covid-safe winter grotto complete with

A poster published during the COVID-19 lockdown as part of the We Are Still Here campaign, to remind audiences that the show was still going on at the Royal Conservatoire of Scotland, albeit online. (Photo: Robert McFadzean; poster design D8)

stockings filled with goodies and hosted by the Principal dressed as Santa. The service was evidently appreciated, being used by more than 40 per cent of students, and was recognised externally as the national winner of Outstanding Contribution to Student Wellbeing in the Herald Scottish Education Awards 2021.

The Conservatoire's performance venues, like theatres, concert halls and cinemas across the country, were dark to public audiences. To make a case for the arts, as well as highlighting the ongoing need to support the next generation of artists, the We Are Still Here campaign was born. A large poster was placed prominently outside the Renfrew Street building informing anyone who passed the red brick building that creativity was still alive inside, although it might not look like it. A piece of spoken word was created. It needed a voice that could express the frustrations and defiance felt by the artists. Alumnus, activist (and Hollywood star) James McAvoy responded immediately. #WeAreStillHere called on people to support the future of young artists and that of the arts itself.

With footage filmed throughout the pandemic, the film featured original music from pianist and composer Fergus McCreadie, a rising star on the European jazz scene, an RCS graduate and scholarship recipient himself. It was layered with James' poetic and stirring vocals that encapsulate how it felt to be part of the arts at that time.

> I'm still here.
> In the wings, out of the limelight, in position, finding my way.
> Searching for meaning, finding a feeling, thought,
> an expression that I can give to you.
> I'm still here.
> Making that moment for you.
> I'm still here.
> Are you?

And, in conclusion, the answer is 'Yes', the Conservatoire is still here. It has endured and more than that, thrived, throughout its 175

CODA

years of metamorphosis from a modest, novel enterprise created to offer Glasgow's citizenry an opportunity for betterment through artistic education into a truly world-leading and international centre of learning.

Little did brothers James and Moses Provan think their Victorian foundling would, in the 21st century, be mentioned in the same breath as the Royal College of Music in London and New York's Juilliard School as one of the top three performing arts education institutions in the world. But that's where it sits, on the eve of its 175th anniversary, ranked Number Three in the world in the 2021 QS World Rankings and Number One in the UK in the 2022 *Complete University Guide.*

> It is ironic to celebrate being 175 years young and recognise the accomplishments of our predecessors when we are slowly emerging from two of the most difficult and challenging academic years in our history. The COVID-19 pandemic devastated students and both academic and professional staff, but in its best traditions, Scotland's national conservatoire has survived and learned from the experience. At the heart of its ethos is a staff that cares passionately about its students, respecting them and their inherent talent.
>
> I am confident that the Royal Conservatoire of Scotland is in good hands and will continue to flourish and contribute to Scotland's society, values and international profile as it embarks on its next 175 years.
>
> Nick Kuenssberg, Chair, Board of Governors

But change is a constant and there is no place to rest and reflect, on laurels or otherwise. The Covid era, playing out as it has at the time of writing in slow, painful detail over the weeks and months of 2020 and 2021, will be absorbed eventually into the rhythm of Conservatoire life. New challenges of a different sort will doubtless emerge, and with them possibilities and opportunities.

The arts, like the human body, change constantly and arts education is required to be responsive and adaptive: 330 billion or our cells are replaced daily; every 24 hours, 1 per cent of us is entirely new and every 7–10 years we really do get a whole new you. What will the 'new

Royal Conservatoire of Scotland' be a decade from now or, indeed, another 175 years on? At this point, who knows with any certainty? That is the challenging, worrying part; in part the science of strategic planning and in part the alchemy of attempting foresight. But it is also the exciting part.

Janette Harkess,
Director of External Relations,
Royal Conservatoire of Scotland

A Note on Source Materials

The research work for this book is based on three different types of source materials. Former Glasgow Athenaeum Secretary, James Lauder's jubilee publication *Glasgow Athenaeum: A Sketch of Fifty Years' Work (1847–1897)* published by the Saint Mungo Press (Glasgow) in 1897 was an invaluable record of the early years of the institution, written at a time when some individuals present at the founding of the institution were still alive.

Primary source materials were also found in the Royal Conservatoire of Scotland's Archives & Collections, and in particular the *Board of Governor's Minute Books*, a handwritten record of the early meetings and discussions which brought the Glasgow Athenaeum into existence.

For more modern sources, personal discussions with alumni and retired staff were most helpful. Quotations from individuals are drawn from direct communication with the author, whereas the spotlights were all contributed by the individuals themselves, in their own unique voices. While most of the spotlights were contributed specifically for this publication, a few have been put together from reminiscences shared with the Conservatoire previously.

Acknowledgements

We are indebted to so many people for the creation of this book. Profound thanks must go to our many alumni, present and retired staff who took the time to contribute their memories, either in quotation or as spotlights. This book would be much poorer without your voices.

Thanks must go to Janette Harkess, who proposed the idea of a publication in the first place as well as contributing the Coda and arranging many of the spotlights. Without her this book would never have happened.

Thanks to the team at Luath, especially Gavin MacDougall, Jennie Renton, Rachael Murray, Lauren Grieve and Eilidh MacLennan, and to Madeleine Mankey. The Marketing and Communications team at the Royal Conservatoire of Scotland must be thanked for their boundless energy and patience, particularly Linda Innes, Linda Robertson and Robbie McFadzean. Very special thanks to Caroline Cochrane for her unwavering support, Kelly Gardiner for saving the manuscript more than once, and Adrian Savage for his assistance with some research.

We must acknowledge our debt to the authors of previous anniversary publications over the past 175 years, and from whose long shadows this book has emerged, in particular James Lauder, Grace Matchett and Frank Spedding. Finally, and most important of all, our thanks must go every member of the wider Conservatoire family past, present and those still to come. This story of passion, resilience and commitment to creativity being integral to life itself, is yours.

Luath Press Limited

committed to publishing well written books worth reading

LUATH PRESS takes its name from Robert Burns, whose little collie Luath (*Gael.*, swift or nimble) tripped up Jean Armour at a wedding and gave him the chance to speak to the woman who was to be his wife and the abiding love of his life. Burns called one of the 'Twa Dogs' Luath after Cuchullin's hunting dog in Ossian's *Fingal*. Luath Press was established in 1981 in the heart of Burns country, and is now based a few steps up the road from Burns' first lodgings on Edinburgh's Royal Mile. Luath offers you distinctive writing with a hint of unexpected pleasures.

Most bookshops in the UK, the US, Canada, Australia, New Zealand and parts of Europe, either carry our books in stock or can order them for you. To order direct from us, please send a £sterling cheque, postal order, international money order or your credit card details (number, address of cardholder and expiry date) to us at the address below. Please add post and packing as follows: UK – £1.00 per delivery address; overseas surface mail – £2.50 per delivery address; overseas airmail – £3.50 for the first book to each delivery address, plus £1.00 for each additional book by airmail to the same address. If your order is a gift, we will happily enclose your card or message at no extra charge.

Luath Press Limited
543/2 Castlehill
The Royal Mile
Edinburgh EH1 2ND
Scotland
Telephone: +44 (0)131 225 4326 (24 hours)
Email: sales@luath.co.uk
Website: www.luath.co.uk